IN SEARCH OF THE IRISH
WOLFHOUND

Irish Greyhound Coat of Arms. 2023.
Created by the author.

IN SEARCH
OF THE
IRISH
WOLFHOUND

OWEN DICKEY

Troubador Publishing Ltd
Unit E2 Airfield Business Park
Harrison Road, Market Harborough
Leicestershire LE16 7UL
Tel: 0116 279 2299
Email: books@troubador.co.uk
Web: www.troubador.co.uk

ISBN 978 1 80514 229 4

British Library Cataloguing in Publication Data.
A catalogue record for this book is available from the British Library.

Printed and bound in Great Britain by 4edge Limited
Typeset in 11pt Garamond Pro by Troubador Publishing Ltd, Leicester, UK

*To all those who would rather
be a wolf than a sheep*

CONTENTS

INTRODUCTION

When I first set out to research this book I have to admit that I did not know exactly what direction I would be headed in. My reason for doing so was one of simple curiosity, I had read in various dog books about the legendary ancestors of the Irish wolfhound, one of the most famous dog breeds of the Middle Ages, and their equally legendary reputation as guards and hunting dogs. Today's breed as we know it is certainly a huge and powerful dog, but most assuredly must be a lot tamer than its warlike predecessor, plus there were many writers who considered the modern wolfhound to be the creation of George Augustus Graham and a pale imitation of the hound of old. I have to admit I knew practically nothing of wolfhound history, ancient or modern, which, when I look back now can only have been a good thing, as I approached the task completely devoid of any blinkers or biases. I do not breed wolfhounds or any allied breed and therefore I did not suffer from *breed blindness* either. Thus, when delving into the breed history I was completely open to all the information I would come across and was perfectly willing to let it stand or fall on its own merits. The evidence would speak for itself.

CHAPTER ONE

THE MODERN BREED

Captain George Augustus Graham, a Scotsman living at Dursley, Rednock, Gloucestershire, England, will forever be famous in canine circles as the creator of the modern Irish wolfhound. He set out in the 1860s' to resuscitate the great wolfdog of Ireland, with definite views as to what that should be, as can be seen from this early breed standard which appeared in an article he wrote for, *The Country* February 24th 1876.

General Appearance and Form – That of a very tall, heavy Scotch deerhound; much more massive and majestic looking; active, and tolerably fast, but somewhat less so than the present breed of deerhound; the neck thick in comparison to his form, very muscular and rather long.

Shape of Head – Very long, but not too narrow, coming to a comparative point; nose not too small, and head gradually getting broader from the same evenly up to the back of the skull; much broader between the ears than that of present deerhound.

Coat – Rough and hard all over body, tail, and legs, and of good length; hair on head long, and rather softer than that on body; that under the jaws to be long and wiry, also that over eyes.

Colour – Black, grey, brindle, red, and fawn, though white and parti-coloured dogs were common, and even preferred in olden times.

Shape and Size of Ears – Small in proportion to size of head, and half erect, resembling those of the best deerhounds; if the dog is of light colour a dark ear is to be preferred.

	Dogs	Bitches
Probable height at shoulder	32in to 35in	28in to 30in
Girth of chest	38in to 44in	32in to 34in
Round forearm	10in to 12in	8in to 9 ½ in
Length of head	12 ½ to 14in	10 ½ to 11 ½ in
Total length	84in to 100in	70in to80in
Weight in lbs	110 to 140	90 to 110

This initial standard was enlarged upon as can be seen from the following standard contained in the book, *Modern Dogs* by Rawdon Briggs Lee, published in 1893 by Horace Cox, London.

THE IRISH WOLFHOUND

The following is the description of the variety as drawn up by the Club:

1. *General appearance.* — The Irish wolfhound should not be quite so heavy or massive as the Great Dane, but more so than the deerhound, which in general type he should otherwise resemble. Of great size and commanding appearance, very muscular, strongly though gracefully built; movements easy and active; head and neck carried high; the tail carried with an upward sweep with a slight curve towards the extremity. The minimum height and weight of dogs should be 31 in., and 120 lb; of bitches 28 in., and 90 lb. Anything below this should be debarred from competition. Great size, including height at shoulder and proportionate length of body, is the desideratum to be aimed at, and it is desired to firmly establish a race that shall average from 32 in., to 34 in., in dogs, showing the requisite power, activity, courage, and symmetry.

2. *Head.* — Long, the frontal bones of the forehead *very* slightly raised, and *very* little indentation between the eyes. Skull, not too broad. Muzzle, long and moderately pointed. Ears, small and greyhound-like in carriage.

3. *Neck.* — Rather long, very strong and muscular, well arched, without dewlap or loose skin about the throat.

4. *Chest.* — Very deep. Breast wide.

5. *Back.* — Rather long than short. Loins, arched.

6. *Tail.* — Long and slightly curved, of moderate thickness and well covered with hair.

7. *Belly*. — Well drawn up.

8. *Fore-quarters*. — Shoulders, muscular, giving breadth of chest, set sloping. Elbows, well under, neither turned inwards nor outwards. *Leg*. — Fore-arm muscular, and the whole leg strong and quite straight.

9. *Hind-quarters*. — Muscular thighs and second thigh long and strong as in the greyhound, and hocks well let down and turning neither in nor out.

10. *Feet*. — Moderately large and round, neither turned inwards nor outwards. Toes well arched and closed. Nails, very strong and curved.

11. *Hair*. — Rough and hard on body, legs, and head; especially wiry and long over eyes and under jaw.

12. *Colour and markings*. — The recognised colours are grey, brindle, red, black, pure white, fawn, or any colour that appears in the deerhound.

13. *Faults*. — Too light or too heavy a head, too highly arched frontal bone; large ears and hanging flat to the face; short neck; full dewlap; too narrow or too broad a chest; sunken or hollow or quite straight back; bent fore-legs; overbent fetlocks; twisted feet; spreading toes; too curly a tail; weak hind-quarters and a general want of muscle; too short in body.

The following is the modern, official breed standard of the Irish wolfhound as laid down by the, Irish Wolfhound Club, founded by Captain Graham in 1876.

STANDARD OF EXCELLENCE

(As amended at the 1981 Annual General Meeting)

General Appearance

The Irish wolfhound is the largest and the tallest of the galloping hounds, it combines power and swiftness with keen sight and in general appearance, very muscular, strongly though gracefully built, movements easy and active, head and neck carried high, the tail carried low with a slight upward sweep towards the extremity.

Head and Skull

Long, the frontal bones of the forehead very slightly raised and very little indentation between the eyes. Skull not too broad. Muzzle long and moderately pointed.

Eyes

Dark.

Ears

Small, greyhound-like in appearance.

Bite

Scissor, level is, however permitted.

Neck

Rather long, very strong and muscular, well arched, without dewlap or loose skin about the throat.

Forequarters

Shoulders muscular, giving breadth of chest, set sloping. Elbows well under, turning neither inwards nor outwards. Leg, forearm muscular and the whole leg strong and quite straight.

Body
Chest, very deep. Breast, wide. Back, rather long than short. Loins arched. Belly well drawn up.

Hindquarters
Muscular thighs and second thighs long and strong as in the greyhound, hocks well let down and turning neither inwards nor outwards.

Feet
Moderately large and round, turning neither inwards nor outwards. Toes well arched and closed. Nails very strong and curved.

Movement
Easy and active.

Tail
Long and slightly curved, of moderate thickness and well covered with hair.

Coat
Rough and hard on body, legs and head, especially wiry and long over eyes and under jaw.

Colour
The recognised colours are grey, brindle, red, black, pure white, fawn, or any colour that appears in the deerhound.

Weight and Size
The minimum height and weight of dogs should be 31 inches and 120 lbs, of bitches 28 inches and 90 lbs. Anything

below this should be debarred from competition. Great size including height at the shoulder and proportionate length of body is the desideratum to be aimed at, and it is desired to firmly establish a breed that shall average 32 to 34 inches in dogs, showing the requisite power, activity and symmetry.

Faults

Too light or heavy a head, too highly arched frontal bone, large ears, ears hanging flat to the face, short neck, full dewlap, too narrow or too broad a chest, sunken, hollow or quite straight back, bent forelegs, over-bent fetlocks, twisted feet, spreading toes, too curly a tail, weak hindquarters and a general want of muscle, too short in body, pink or liver coloured eyelids, lips and nose any colour other than black, very light eyes, coat soft or woolly.

Note

Male animals should have two apparently normal testicles fully descended into the scrotum.

LIST OF POINTS IN ORDER OF MERIT

1. Typical. The Irish wolfhound should not be quite so heavy or massive as the Great Dane, but more so than the deerhound, which in general type he should otherwise resemble.
2. Great size and commanding appearance.
3. Movement easy and active.
4. Head long and level, carried high.
5. Forelegs heavily boned, quite straight, elbows well set under.
6. Thighs long and muscular, second thighs well-muscled, stifles slightly bent.
7. Body long well ribbed up, with ribs well sprung and great.

Coat rough and hard, specially wiry and long over the eyes and under the jaw. Breadth across the hips.

8. Loins arched, belly well drawn up.
9. Ears small and greyhound-like in carriage.
10. Feet moderately large and round, toes close, well arched.
11. Neck long, well arched and very strong.
12. Chest very deep, moderately broad.
13. Shoulders muscular, set sloping.
14. Tail long and slightly curved.
15. Eyes dark.

Note

The above in no way alters the, *"Standard of Excellence,"* which must in all cases be rigidly adhered to, they simply give the various points in order of merit. If in any case they appear at variance with the, *"Standard of Excellence,"* it is the latter which is correct.

Comparing Graham's original standard with the modern one is quite reassuring in that the breed club seems to be adhering to the founder's goals. Movement being, *easy and active,* is a very important point. Many wolfhounds today are truly enormous and breeders must take great care that they are not breeding infirmity into this giant of dogdom. It is too easy to get carried away by the quest for greater size, meanwhile forgetting about the health and happiness of the dog, some large breeds are positively geriatric by the time they are six years old, a sad comment on short-sighted breeders. The Irish wolfhound is probably the healthiest of the giant breeds, due I would say, to the large amount of deerhound blood flowing through its veins, coursing hounds have always been among the most genetically perfect and physically sound varieties of canine.

The Dog of Today

The Irish wolfhound is without a doubt one of the most physically impressive dogs in the world today, while all of them are very large dogs, some are truly enormous and definitely would not appear out of place in the castles and forts of the medieval period. Their shaggy coats, noble bearing and subdued colours stir thoughts of mountain, moorland and peat bog as their natural haunts and we get visions of bearded clansmen out for a hunt with their enormous charges held on slips until the opportune moment. But, to return to the present, as well as being a real traffic stopper, the modern dog has probably one of the best temperament's in the canine world, they are a docile, phlegmatic breed with an easy going attitude and are never given to senseless barking. So how then, did we arrive at today's dog?

History and Development

The wolfhound of today is basically the creation of a Scotsman, Captain George Augustus Graham and a few like-minded individuals. Graham was of the opinion that the original Irish hound was simply a larger more powerful version of the Scottish deerhound and put forward various arguments in support of his theory. These appeared in an article published in, *The Country*, of February 24, 1876.

Graham stated that there was enough blood of the true breed remaining in Ireland, (though in one or two places only), and in the deerhound to allow the complete resuscitation of the Irish hound. So, it would appear that Graham's early breeding attempts centred on dogs from Ireland, which he considered likely descendants of the hounds of old, crossed with deerhounds. However, later in the same piece Graham mentions an earlier enthusiast, Richardson, who himself had attempted to revive the hound of old and from whose stock Graham considered the purest remnants of the Irish hound to descend, so it was these descendants of an earlier attempt at resuscitation blended with the deerhound which were the cornerstone of Graham's breeding program.

Dr John Henry Walsh, *Stonehenge*, in his book on dogs includes the same article by Graham but goes on to state that Great Dane blood had been liberally used in the creation of the Irish wolfhound, as the new breed became known. This was in order to increase size and mass and cites three examples; Colonel Garnier's Hecla, Mr. Townsend's Lufan of Ivanhoe and Mr. Laloe's McMahon all sired by Cedric the Saxon, a fawn coloured Great Dane. Certainly, some early examples of wolfhounds were very Dane-like in appearance and today it is a generally acknowledged fact that Great Dane blood was used to develop the modern wolfhound. Another breed said to be used was the Russian wolfhound or Borzoi, but there is little evidence to support this and there is reference to a Pyrenean wolfdog, whatever that was, in the early years of the breed's development.

Edward Ash, in his, *The Practical Dog Book* of 1931 was in no doubt when he stated:

'This remarkable dog, the Irish wolfhound, is a breed produced by the skilful blending of Great Dane and deerhound.'

Therefore, to sum up, we can say the modern Irish wolfhound is comprised of the following to varying degrees:

Blood from some large, rough-haired dogs bred down from Richardson's earlier attempts at reviving the great Irish wolfdog.

The Scottish deerhound

The Great Dane

Graham formed the, Irish Wolfhound Club, in 1876 and in 1886 the breed was recognised by the English Kennel Club.

Sporting Aspects

That Graham and his cohorts succeeded in their quest to produce a larger more powerful version of the Scottish deerhound is obvious today and it is obvious from their writings that this is what they considered the original Irish wolfhound to be. With that in mind I would like to take a look at the sporting aspect of today's Irish wolfhound.

The Irish greyhound, or wolfdog of old, is most famously regarded as a wolf hunter, though no doubt it was also adept at hunting the other game found in Ireland and Britain such as deer and wild boar. Indeed the fame of the breed spread far and wide and one contemporary writer described them as the greatest hunting dogs in Europe. So, what of the modern wolfhound, how do they measure up in the field of honour? Speaking personally, I have no idea, so I am going to quote from two definite authorities in the field of coursing, M.H. *Dutch* Salmon, author of, *Gazehounds & Coursing*, and E.G. Walsh, author of, *Lurchers & Longdogs*, both men having bred and kept coursing dogs all their lives and having used the same to hunt all manner of game.

To refer first to Walsh, he quotes an American who did a lot of coyote hunting between the first and second World Wars, whose preference for dogs was; first, the greyhound, then the mixed blood greyhound, next the deerhound, the Borzoi and the hybrid between them and lastly the Irish wolfhound,

'…not for his speed, for he has none, but only if he was a fighter.'

Another correspondent from America stated,

'As regards the pure breeds, the deerhound and Borzoi are ideally suited for coyotes but so few are hunted that most individuals are found lacking, either in speed or desire. I don't believe a single kennel in America today is currently raising either deerhounds or Borzoi primarily for hunting. As for the Irish wolfhound, I've yet to see one that was more than one stride better than useless on any game.'

An Australian whose quarry included kangaroo, pigs and foxes had this to say,

'I have tried greyhounds but they are no good in rough country, too easily hurt. Deerhounds are the tops; gave up Borzois after five years, too temperamental. Wolfhounds can be very game but are not fast enough. Afghans are a write-off, too much coat and no brains. Salukis are a lovely hound, fast and tough but they are the only breed of dog I could not control, could not get 'through' to them.'

Salmon mentions Leon Almirall who assessed coyote hounds in *Canines and Coyotes* and who rated the greyhound, Scottish deerhound and Borzoi highly and in that order but had little good to say about the Irish wolfhound, stating that the wolfhound was comparatively slow and cumbersome afoot. Salmon himself states,

'As a matter of opinion I'd have to say that the Irish wolfhound is the least useful of the coursing breeds today. In being so large the Irish hound pays too great a price in speed and agility to be of much use in coursing hare, fox or even coyote.'

Not exactly glowing with praise, but Salmon does concede some praise later in his book,

'In defence of the Irish wolfhound I must say that even the veteran rural hunters, most of whom have experimented with the breed, concede that the Irish wolfhound is a natural at the catch, killing coyote with ease and rarely getting cut in the process.' Although, 'Few, in their experience or mine, can catch one alone.'

But, again admits,

'There are exceptions.'

From the foregoing it would seem that the sporting ability of the wolfhound is seriously limited, with the major criticisms being a lack of speed and agility, though it is interesting to note that these hunting men considered the breed to be quite courageous when they were able to engage the quarry. This I found to be a pleasant surprise. I know from conversations with various lurchermen here in Ireland that few lurchers make really good single-handed fox killers, many will sometimes have a go but after being bitten soon fight shy and never seem able to close with the fox. Now this is an opponent with an average weight of 14 to 18 lbs, whereas coyotes weigh from 20 to 50 lbs and can dish out punishment in an equally inflated fashion, so for Irish wolfhounds to make a good showing at such an opponent is to me pretty impressive, even if they do find it very difficult to make the initial catch. The crux of the matter seems to be the wolfhound's size and the simple fact of the matter is that a dog of his stature is just not meant to hunt rabbit, hare or fox, any of which can easily outmanoeuvre him More legitimate prey would be coyote and deer, indeed D.B. Plummer in his book, *Sighthounds, Longdogs & Lurchers,* mentions a brace of wolfhounds that had been used to hunt deer in England and seemingly had little difficulty in pulling down the largest fallow bucks. Wild pig would seem another suitable quarry, but in America, Australia and New Zealand where this is a popular sport, the pig hunt is carried out almost exclusively with the bull breeds and their crosses.

The following is an excerpt from an article by Freeman Lloyd on Scottish deerhounds and Irish wolfhounds from the *American Kennel Gazette* August 31st 1931.

'Wolf hunting is still much practiced in western Canada, and from intimate conversations with those who keep dogs for the purpose of running down prairie wolves, (coyotes), it appeared that the type of the large Scottish deerhound is preferred to the larger Irish dogs – strong as oxen but not possessing quite the turn of speed of a 30 inches at the shoulder, 100-pound weight deerhound. Over and over I have heard the prairie dogs described as Irish wolfhounds by farmers of Manitoba and farther west. But, as Irish wolfhounds, they were comparatively puny in height, weight, bone and power.'

Although not intending to, Lloyd was in effect reinforcing the opinion of practical coursing men who consider the wolfhound too big to be of much use in the hunting field.

To sum up then, the Irish wolfhound still seems to possess the hunting instinct, but his enormous size works against him in the course, making him inferior to smaller, more athletic breeds such as the greyhound and deerhound.

Companion Dog

But what the modern wolfhound lacks in sporting prowess he seems to more than make up for in his role as a faithful and loving companion. The following is from an article by a Mr. McAleenan, one of the first and most important fanciers of the breed in America.

'My old dog Finn was with me constantly, and in the long walks we have taken together over the sand dunes close by the sea he would walk at my side and for miles would hold my hand balanced between his great jaws. I thought this was peculiar to him, but I was new in my experience with the breed then, and have since discovered that this is a trait, an instinct, a habit with the breed in general. No other dog can come so close to the understanding and kindly companionship that exists sometimes between humans as this dog can. A giant in stature, a lamb in disposition, and a lion in courage, affectionate and intelligent, thoroughly reliable and dependable at all times, as a companion and guard he is perfection.'

High praise indeed, but praise which is repeated over and over again by others who have owned the breed. Of course one always has to view plaudits for any breed in the light of who is bestowing them, a breeder of wolfhounds is not likely to speak ill of them, but the following is a true story which occurred during the First World War that I believe portrays the Irish wolfhound in a truly noble light.

- This picture shows the front page of the publication, *Le Miroir*, of Sunday, June 17th, 1917.
- There is no article in the magazine about it but below the picture is the statement:

Front page of Le Miroir. 1917.

'A soldier and his dog who were wounded by the same shell. At the Brimont fort this liaison agent and his dog, who assisted him in his missions, were wounded at the same time. In hospital, the faithful animal refused to be separated from his master. The same nurse treats both of them each day.'

Le Miroir was a dedicated war news periodical which published many photographs of war scenes with a few articles.

In the following article, written over a year later in *Country Life*, November 1918, we find out the story behind the picture.

BALLY SHANNON – DOG of WAR
By WALTER A. DYER
Author of *'Pierrot, Dog of Belgium,' 'The Dogs of Boytown,'* etc.

I visited him in the sheep-fold of Central Park, New York, where he was being kept for the British officers who had brought him over. And this is the story they tell of him:

Bally Shannon had been, like them, a soldier in France. No ordinary ambulance helper was he, but an over-the-top fighter. Ten wounded men he saved by dragging them out of No Man's Land. Then came a bursting shell and Bally Shannon and his master were both wounded. They were sent home on a hospital ship, and in mid-Channel the ship was torpedoed by a German submarine.

The torpedo did its work well, and the ship went down with nearly all on board. Only three men were saved – Bally Shannon's master and two others. They managed to scramble on top of a barely floating piece of wreckage.

Then came the brave dog, swimming strongly in spite of his wounds, and begged to be taken aboard. But the piece of wreckage would not have withstood his additional weight, and his master was forced to order him to keep away.

Without so much as a look of reproach Bally Shannon obeyed. All night he swam about the rude raft, only resting his chin upon it when nearly exhausted. In the morning they were picked up.

When I visited the dog he was nearly well, though his master, alas, had succumbed to his wounds and the exposure. I spoke his name, but not in the tone with which one addresses a spaniel. He came to the edge of the enclosure and raised himself to his full height, resting his forepaws on the top of the fence. His head was level with mine.

I thought I had never seen so magnificent an animal. All sinew and brawn, powerful, built on lines of speed, he stood there and received my homage. I placed my hand reverently on his broad, shaggy head and let it slide down his muzzle. He took it for an instant in his mouth with the utmost gentleness. I was a stranger to Bally Shannon, but he was the friend of man.

And I looked into his eyes – great, honest, intelligent eyes, utterly human. "I know what you did, Bally Shannon," said I. "You're a better man than I am, Gunga Din."

I saw in those eyes the devotion and unquestioning courage that had upheld him that dark night in the Channel water. I saw in them the heritage of his noble race, the spirit of Bran and Luath, of peerless Gelert and the faithful dog of Aughrim. I saw in them, too, the mystery of the dog's wonderful gift for attaching himself to humankind.

There are people who do not like dogs. I wish they might see noble Bally Shannon and might have the courage frankly to approach him. I know not why God gave the dog this spark of divinity that has made him kin to man. I only know this – that when we shall have learned from the dog the beauty of his virtues of honesty, fidelity, and courage, the world will be a better place for us all, and Hun and savage and Turk will be driven off the face of the earth as the wolves were driven out of Ireland.'

The Mentor Association, New York, dedicated one of its *The Mentor* publications to *Our Friend the Dog*. This was Vol. 6, No. 16, of October 1st, 1918 and contained this picture of Bally Shannon (the same as in the *Country Life* article but with the background left in):

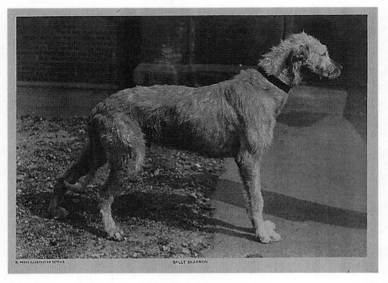

Ballyshannon. 1918.

On the back of the picture it reads:

'The Mentor is fortunate in being able to reproduce the picture of a hero of heroes, one that has proved twice over the valiant stuff that dogs are made of. Bally Shannon, an Irish wolfhound, was taken by a British officer into the trenches, and served there as a Red Cross dog until wounded in the left shoulder by a shell. His master was also wounded, and together they were invalided home. Crossing the English Channel, the hospital ship on which they rode was torpedoed in the night. The officer and two others found refuge on a piece of wreckage, but there was no room for Bally Shannon, and his great weight would have submerged the others. When he attempted to get aboard the floating timbers, his master warned him back with a gentle word of explanation. And Bally understood. Thereafter he made no effort to climb out of the icy waters; only when he grew over-weary he came close and rested his shaggy head and fore-paws on the edge of the improvised raft until he had strength to go on paddling about in the dark and the cold. At daylight they were saved, and later the dog and his master came to America to recuperate from wounds and exposure. Since then, though not fully recovered, Bally has again been a dog of service, helping the shepherd in Central Park, New York, to guard the sheep that crop the grass, tame work enough after succouring wounded soldiers on the battlefield. But his friends' hope a life among peaceful surroundings will some day soften the sorrow of his war-troubled eyes.'

You will note that the former article says Bally Shannon's owner died of his wounds, whereas the latter states he came with the dog to New York to recuperate. Whether Bally Shannon's owner survived or not I do not know, but I think the reader will agree that such a dog would warrant the very best of care for the rest of his days.

And from as recently as 2008 we have the story of the Irish wolfhound, RK, who along with his pal, Deke, the English mastiff, saved their owner from a black bear attack in the Sequoia Mountains of California. The fifty-eight year old woman, Allena Hansen, was walking near her remote ranch house when the bear attacked, she called for her dogs and after a ferocious fight the bear was driven off. Allena suffered severe injuries to her head and face, (there are pictures on the internet to show just how severe), but survived and following extensive plastic surgery it would be hard to tell the attack ever happened.

In summary, the modern Irish wolfhound is a huge, shaggy, impressive dog with a wonderful temperament and a devoted following. They are probably the healthiest of the very large dog breeds and still have the instinct to chase game given the chance. I admit I am a fan and wish the breed and its followers nothing but success for the future.

CHAPTER TWO

THE IRISH HOUND IN HISTORY, MYTH AND LEGEND

The greyhound! The great hound! The graceful of limb!
Rough fellow! Tall fellow! Swift fellow, and slim!
Let them sound through the earth, let them sail o'er the sea,
They will light on none other more ancient than thee!

In this chapter I have decided to begin at the beginning, so to speak, and gradually work my way forwards in time until the most recent plausible accounts of the existence of the Irish greyhound. First of all, I should say that the old, Irish hound was known by a variety of names such as: Irish wolfdog, wolf-dog of Ireland, great Irish hound, greyhound of Ireland and most commonly, Irish greyhound.

The earliest account I came across in my research was a mention of, 'huge, swift, hounds', which were used by Celts as war-dogs when they sacked Delphi, Greece, in 279 BC. This certainly seemed promising, but I am afraid it did not stand up to closer scrutiny. There are only two sources for the Celtic raids into northern Greece at that time; Pausanias and the later Justin, of these only Pausanias is considered reliable. However, neither account mentions dogs of any kind being used by the invaders, and indeed the Celts were also unsuccessful in their attack on Delphi, being repulsed by the Greek coalition.

We must turn to legend for our first account and the tales of Cuchulainn, the 'Hound of Ulster', whose heroics are dated to early in the first century AD.

As a boy, Cuchulainn was known as Setanta, he was what the Greeks would have referred to as a 'demi-god', being both superhuman and yet mortal. His mother was a mortal who had been whisked off to the world of the Danaans, (a supernatural race who had inhabited Ireland thousands of years before), by their chief, Lugh Lamhfada. A year later following an extensive search, the child Setanta was found at one of the 'fairy mounds' in the Boyne valley, (possibly Newgrange), and brought back to the seat of the King of Ulster, Conchobor Mac Nessa, at Emain Macha, near present day Armagh, (now known as Navan Fort).

A few years later, King Conchobor and his entourage rode out to attend a feast being held by Culann, a famous smith; Setanta had been at play when the party left and so was very late in departing. King Conchobor and his attendants duly arrived at Culann's and were ushered inside the hall where they began to feast.

As darkness approached and in true dramatic fashion, Culann asked the King if all of his party were inside, as he was about to release his great hound who guarded the property during the hours of darkness.

"I have a savage hound," Culann said. "Three chains are needed to hold him, with three men on each chain. Let him loose," he ordered, "to guard our cattle and other stock. Shut the gate of the enclosure."

Soon Setanta arrived and the hound started out for him. But he still attended to his game: he tossed his ball up and threw his hurling stick after it and struck it; the length of his stroke never varied. Then he would cast his javelin after both and catch it before it fell. His game never faltered although the hound was tearing toward him. Conchobor and his people were in such anguish at this that they couldn't stir. They were sure they couldn't reach him alive, even if the enclosure gate was open. The hound sprang. Cuchulainn tossed the ball aside and the stick with it and tackled the hound with his two hands: he clutched the hound's throat-apple in one hand and grasped its back with the other. He smashed it against the nearest pillar and its limbs leaped from their sockets.

(According to another version he threw his ball into its mouth and so tore out its entrails.)

Then the Ulstermen rose up to meet him, some of them over the rampart, others through the gate of the enclosure. They carried him to Conchobor's bosom. They gave a great cry of triumph that the son of the King's sister had escaped death.

Culann stood in his house.

"You are welcome, boy, for your mother's heart's sake. But for my own part I did badly to give this feast. My life is a waste, and my household like a desert, with the loss of my hound! He guarded my life and my honour," he said; "a valued servant, my hound, taken from me. He was shield and shelter for our goods and herds. He guarded all our beasts at home or out in the fields."

"That doesn't matter," the boy said. "I'll rear you a pup from the same pack. Until that hound grows up to do his work, I will be your hound, and guard yourself and your beasts. And I will guard all Murtheimne Plain. No herd or flock will leave my care unknown to me."

"Cuchulainn shall be your name, the Hound of Culann," Cathbad said.

"I like that for a name!" Cuchulainn said.

(From, *The Tain,* translated by Thomas Kinsella)

Although a legend we could take the following inferences from this story. Firstly, that there were large dogs in ancient Ireland, secondly, that one of their uses was to guard home and property and thirdly, that they could be extremely ferocious. Of course we cannot say that the dog in question was an Irish greyhound, the description could apply equally to a mastiff, but it is an interesting snippet nevertheless.

Around this same period a hound named Ailbe became so famous throughout Ireland that the rulers of Connaught, King Ailill and Queen Medb, made an offer to his owner Mac Datho of:

'Three score hundred milk cows at once and a chariot with two horses and as much again at the end of the year.'

A similar offer was made by King Conchobor of Ulster, whose province in those days seemed to be in a constant state of enmity with Connaught.

'Ailbe, his famous cunning splendid hound,
From whom is the renowned plain of Ailbe'.

It was said that Ailbe could run through Leinster in a day. The owner, realising he could not accept one province's offer without offending the other was in a state of flux, so following his wife's advice he promised the hound to both parties and arranged them to come on the same day. Tensions were running so high that a battle broke out between the rival kingdoms; to let himself off the hook Mac Datho released the hound stating that Ailbe could chose who he would side with himself. The dog chose Ulster and gave chase to the Connaught king's chariot, seizing the chariot pole, whereupon the charioteer moved forward and decapitated the hound, though the jaws held their grip from Ballaghmoon in Kildare to Farbill in Westmeath. At Farbill the head dropped as they crossed a ford, there afterwards known as Ath Cind Chon, 'Hound's Head Ford.'

From the story of Ailbe we can say the dog in question had great stamina, was fast and had a powerful bite, and it is the quality of speed which indicates a breed other than a mastiff.

In returning to recorded history, mention is made of the dogs of Britain by Lacus Curtius Strabo (63 BC – 23 AD), in his, *Geography*.

> 'It bears grain, cattle, gold, silver and iron. These things
> accordingly are exported from the island, as also hides and
> slaves and dogs that are by nature suited to the purposes of
> the chase; the Celti, (Gauls), however, use both these and the
> native dogs for the purposes of war too.'

So, it would seem that even early in the first century British hunting dogs were considered a valuable export and if one reads between the lines further information can be garnered. That these dogs were efficient hunting dogs but could also be used as war-dogs would tend to rule out scent hounds as they seldom saw use on the battlefield. Likewise the sleek greyhound used to hunt the hare would have been of little use. Again, I believe only the following three breeds could be referred to here, the

Irish greyhound, the mastiff, or the forerunner of the Scottish deerhound. I feel it necessary to point out here that the mastiff of old was much lighter in build and much more athletic than today's breed.

Another reference from Irish lore comes from the, *Tain Bo Flidais*, which details an internal dispute inside the province of Connaught. Caused yet again by the launching of a cattle raid in pursuit of one special animal, the white cow known as the, 'Maol'. The following excerpt is from, *The Glenmasan Manuscript* version.

'As to the Gamhanraidh. After they heard of the fate of their lord, they did not keep their compact with the troops, but proceeded to avenge him. Donald Yellowlocks was the first to overtake, with his pack of hounds along with him. And he set loose upon them a powerful, ferocious, strange wolf-dog with fifty fierce, courageous dogs along with it. These eagerly attacked the hosts so that the men of Ireland were forced forthwith to face them because of the furious and dangerous grip with which the wolf-dogs seized them. They and Donald's soldiers were with ardour destroying and beheading each warrior of the men of Ireland whom they fell upon. Fergus and the Dubloinges went to shield the men of Ireland from them, and he and the wolf-dogs fought forthwith. Fergus went in his chariot, and when a specially dangerous and powerful wolf-dog of Donald's saw him in the chariot it made a fierce and very sudden spring at him. Fergus with Fergarbh, his charioteer, stood watchfully to meet the attack. The dog disregarding their weapons sprang into the chariot. When Fergus raised his weapon to deliver a blow, the chariot gave way under him, for it was not able to sustain the weight of the three powerful individuals at one and the same time, and its wheels and shafts and axles broke right away. When Fergus could not obtain a firm foothold in the chariot he leapt out, carrying his weapons with him. And when his warriors followed him the dog made an angry, fierce, and venomous rush with her teeth at Fergarbh. She caught the small of his body, (his neck), firmly in her big-fanged, open mouth, and tore his head from his body. And when she failed to find Fergus near she seized on the horses, attacked them furiously, and killed them forthwith. When the men of Ireland saw Fergus leaving his chariot unsupported, panic almost seized them. Donald's people, and the dogs, and the first muster of the heroes of the Gamhanraidh slew a great many of the followers of Medb, and Ailill, and Fergus in that scare, and wrought many losses and disasters upon them. Fergus felt shamed at the check he experienced, and turned back again to the broken chariot, which he had abandoned. He found his charioteer and horses mangled by Donald's dog. He gave a look of triumph at her, and grasped his spear to crush her. He made a quick, well-aimed cast at her, when the spear entered her head, and, after piercing it, fixed itself in the ground, so that her life left her in that spot.'

When the bard composed a verse after the battle he did not fail to mention the role played by Donald's wolfdog.

'Donald's hound sped from his castle,
With fifty relentless hounds following;
She destroyed the prince's stately chariot,
She slew his truly generous charioteer.
Fergus killed the slim hound,
With the polished spear that pierced her head
On the field above the glen,'

Returning again to Celtic legend and the, *Fenian Cycle*, which tells the stories of Finn Mac Cumhaill and the Fianna, his warrior brotherhood, we find once again mention of famous hounds. Each warrior of the Fianna was permitted.

'…two hounds and two keen beagles,'

Whilst Finn himself had.

'…three hundred hounds and puppy hounds two hundred;'

In his role as Master of Hounds for King Cormac.

'Now he whom Cormac had for chief of the household
and for stipendiary master of the hounds was Finn, son of
Cumhaill; for the primest leader that the King of Ireland had
was the master of the hounds always.'

Finn's principal hunting dogs were Bran and Sceolang; they also magically happened to be his cousins. Other dogs appearing less often were Lomair and Adnuall, (sweet of sound), which would seem to indicate he was a baying type of scent hound, fitting in with the beagle reference in the legend. His favourite was the bitch, Bran, who,

'…always killed more men or beasts than Finn.'

Truly, an animal to be respected! Bran, has been erroneously translated by past writers as, 'mountain torrent', when in fact it is Old Irish for 'raven', a bird associated with death throughout the Celtic world.

In the, *Lay of the Enchanted Pigs*, we have an account of Bran in action, hunting wild boar which, had once been warriors, changed into their current form by a wizard for the express purpose of killing Finn's hounds.

'Finn of the Fianna was amazed
At seeing each pig as tall as a deer;
One pig before them of boisterous mien,
Blacker was she than smith's coals;
Longer than an erect mast
Were the bristles of her face and ears;
Like that of a brake was the colour
Of the hair of her eyelids and old brow.

Bran broke forth from her leash
And left the hands of the king.

She takes the pig by the neck
And assumes the difficult task.
She takes the pig by the neck,
The hold was the hold of a foe;
She did not suffer the pig to escape
And never became breathless.'

On a mountain in Tyrone, near Newtownstewart, is said to be a mark in the rock known as, 'The Track of the Foot of Bran, Hound of Finn Mac Cumhaill'. Bran is said to be buried at Carnawaddy, (carn an mhadra – cairn of the dog), near Omeath, Co. Louth. It is also thought that Lough Brin in Co. Kerry is named after Bran.

In the stories recorded by James Macpherson in his, *Fingal*, of 1762, part of, *The Poems of Ossian* (stories obviously based on the Irish legend), we again have references to Fingal's, (Finn's), hounds.

"Call," said Fingal, "call my dogs, the long-bounding sons of the chase. Call white-breasted Bran, and the surly strength of Luath!"

And again;

'A thousand dogs fly off at once, gray-bounding through the heath. A deer fell by every dog; three by the white-breasted Bran. He brought them, in their flight, to Fingal, that the joy of the king might be great! One deer fell at the tomb of Ryno.'

It is interesting to note that Bran was male in Macpherson's tales. Another favourite dog of Fingal's was Conbec,

'...no hound but Conbec did ever sleep in the one bed with Finn.'

At Traig Chonbicce, named after the event, Conbec was treacherously drowned by Goll, one of Fingal's rivals, causing him great sorrow:

'Piteous to me was Conbec's cruel death,
Conbec of perfect symmetry,
I have not seen a more expert of foot
In the wake of wild boar or stag.
A pang to me was Conbec's tragic fate,
Conbec of the hoarse deep voice;
Never have I seen one more expert of foot
At killing of a buck without delay
A pang to me was Conbec's death
Over the high, green billows,
His cruel death was a cause of strife,
His fate was most pitiful.'

'I have never heard the voice of a hound a-hunting on plain,
on bog or spreading slope, since I parted with my bold hound,
but that woe would come upon my heart.'

Fingal/Finn's son, Ossian, the famed bard and poet is credited
with composing the following verse about his father's hounds:

'An eye of sloe, with ear not low
With horse's breast, with depth of chest,
With breadth of loin and curve in groin.
And nape set far behind the head;
Such were the dogs that Fingal bred.'

It is related that when Ossian returned from the fairy world of, Tír
na Nóg, he met St. Patrick and was converted to Christianity, but
had a question for the saint.

'To the son of Cumhaill and the chiefs of the Fianna it is
sweeter to hear the voice of hounds than to seek mercy. O, son
of Calpurn, wilt thou allow to go to Heaven my own dog and
greyhound?'

In *The Annals of the Four Masters*, it is recorded that in AD 9, the
King, Crimhthann Niadhnairg, undertook a famous expedition
and brought back great treasures among which were:

'...two greyhounds, with a silver chain between them, which
chain was worth three hundred cumhals; with many other
precious articles.'

Around 50 AD, the sons of Uisnech fled from Ulster to Alba,
(Scotland), taking one hundred and fifty hounds with them, many
no doubt, Irish greyhounds. Indeed the Scots, (Ulstermen), went

on to form their own kingdom in what would become Scotland and the Irish hounds would have a direct impact on Scottish history as the following account taken from Holinshed's, *Historie of Scotland*, printed in 1586 will explain:

'And shortlie after the return of these ambassadors into their countrie, divers young gentlemen of the Pictish nobilitie repaired unto King Crathlint, to hunt and make merie with him; but when they should depart homewards, perceiving that the Scotish dogs did farre excel theirs, both in fairnesse, swiftnesse, hardiness, and also in long standing up and holding out, they got diverse both dogs and bitches of the best kinds for breed to be given them by the Scottish Lords; and yet not so contented, they stole one belonging to the king from his keeper, being more esteemed of him than all the others which he had about him. The master of the leash being informed hereof, pursued after them which had stolen that dog, thinking indeed to have taken him from them; but they not willing to part with him, fell at altercation, and in the end chanced to strike the master of the leash through with their horsespeares that he died presentlie: whereupon noise and crie being raised in the countrie by his servants, diverse of the Scots, as they were going home from hunting, returned and falling upon the Picts to revenge the death of their fellow, there ensued a shrewd bickering betwixt them, so that of the Scots there died three score gentlemen, besides a great number of the commons, not one of them understanding, (till all was done), what the matter meant. Of the Picts there were about a hundred slaine. This circumstance led to a bloody war betwixt the two nations.'

This was a war the Scots were to win, when by AD 288, the Pictish kingdom partly collapsed and partly became absorbed, leading eventually to the country becoming known as Scotland.

Moving on to the late Roman period of 391 AD, the Roman Consul, Quintus Aurelius Symmachus, sent a letter of thanks to his brother Flavinius.

'In order to win the favour of the Roman people for our Quaestor you have been a generous and diligent provider of novel contributions to our solemn shows and games as is proven by your gift of seven Scottish dogs. All Rome viewed them with wonder, and fancied they must have been brought hither in iron cages. For such a gift I render you the greatest possible thanks.'

The Scotti, to the Romans were the inhabitants of Ireland and thus these were Irish dogs and more likely than not examples of the Irish greyhound. The Romans would have been familiar with the mastiff and the greyhound, or vertragus, as they called it, but the Irish dogs were evidently of a different breed and yet formidable enough to have performed in the Circus; the great hound fits the bill.

About the year 400, a Christian youth, by the name of Patricius, was carried off into slavery by Irish raiders from his home in Britain. He spent the next six years in Ulster serving as a shepherd, tradition says around the area of Slemish Mountain, in Co. Antrim. Finally deciding to make his escape, having been called by the Lord, Patricius had a dream that a ship would be waiting to take him at a certain harbour. On arrival he found a ship from Gaul in port, whose captain was there for a cargo of hunting dogs. This in itself would lead one to believe that the Gauls were after the great Irish greyhounds, otherwise why make the trip to Ireland. Patricius, or to give him his modern name, Patrick, had no money to pay for his passage and was to be turned away.

However, once aboard ship, the hounds became unsettled and aggressive, being almost impossible to manage, Patrick spoke soothing words to the dogs calming them down and as a result the captain gave him passage, provided he tend to the hounds. After a stormy voyage the ship arrived in Gaul, though not in port but at an uninhabited stretch of coast. The crew and the hounds were famished from want of food and water and so set off inland with some of the hounds on a hunting/foraging foray. They must have been in dire straits for Patrick prayed to God for food. Shortly afterwards a sounder of wild pigs appeared and lingered long enough for the crew with the aid of the hounds to kill several, providing ample meat for themselves and the hounds. Patrick was henceforth treated as one of the crew, eventually making his way back to Britain and from there, once again to Ireland in 432, and in due course becoming our patron saint.

A further reference to Patrick comes from the, *Leabhar Breac*, or *Speckled Book*, compiled around the early 15th century by Murchadh Riabhach O'Cuindlis, recording an event which took place on Patrick's return to Ireland.

> 'Patrick went afterwards in his boat to Inverslany, and there
> came upon him Dichu son of Trechem, and he set against
> him a fierce hound which he had…Patrick made the sign of
> the cross of the Lord against it, and he chanted the prophetic
> verse…and the hound stopt and was unable to stir.'

In the summer of 637, the battle of Magh Rath, (Moira, in modern day County Down), took place, said to be the largest battle in Irish history, lasting seven days. It was committed to the written word sometime in the 12th century. The battle was between the High King Domhnall and his foster-son Congal Claen, King of Ulster, it was a truly all Ireland affair with the forces of Connaught, Leinster and Munster ranged against Ulster with some Scottish and possibly other British allies. Congal according to the written account came up with an unusual method of testing his warriors' mettle.

'The scheme he adopted for proving every true Ultonian, and for testing every foreigner was this, each of them respectively was to go in to him to the principal apartment in his tent, while a fierce and terrible man, with a black, fearful javelin with a hard leather head, in readiness to thrust, was at the one jamb (of the door of the tent), and a furious, swift, fearful hound at the other jamb, having on him a thick iron collar, fastened to a strong pole to keep him; a sturdy boy beside him to check or incite him; and when an Ultonian or foreigner would come between them, where he could be attacked, the man with the hard leather-headed javelin was to make a thrust at him from the one jamb, and the hound, in like manner, to spring at him from the other jamb. Should the man to be chosen turn back, or take fright at the attack of the man with the spear, or at the dire onset of the hound exposing his teeth and extending his jaws to tear or hold him fast, he was taken and fettered without delay. But he who had passed the horrors of this mode of trial, without panic or dismay, was left without restraint. The first man, whose courage was, before all, tested by this plan, was Dubhdiadh, the Druid, for he was stopped and taken on the highest pole (ridge pole) of the tent, having been panic stricken and driven to distraction at the horror of this attack. In short there was not found a man who did not shrink and fly from it except Ferdoman the Bloody, the son of Imoman, but he cleft the hound's jaws and cut in twain its heart in its breast with his warlike sword, and immediately after slew without mercy with his lance the man who was armed with the spear at the other jamb,'

The Book of Leinster, completed around the end of the 12th century contains the story of, *How Ronan Slew His Son*, which, it is thought refers to events in the 10th century. The son, Mael Fothartaig, went to Scotland to avoid his lustful stepmother.

'Thereupon he went with fifty warriors into Scotland. He found great welcome with the King of Scotland. He had hounds for hares, hounds for boars, hounds for deer. But Doilin and Daithlenn, two hounds of Mael Fothartaig, would kill every quarry in turn before them. Every host that was routed before the king of Scotland, and every fight that was won, it was the doing of Mael Fothartaig.'

Our next mention is in, *The Heimskringla*, composed around 1225, by the poet and historian, Snorri Sturluson. We learn of an Irish hound called Vige, acquired by Olaf Tryggvason, who as King of Norway, reigned from 995 to 1000 AD.

'While Olaf was in Ireland he was once on an expedition which went by sea. As they required to make a foray for provisions on the coast, some of his men landed, and drove down a large herd of cattle to the strand. Now a peasant came up, and entreated Olaf to give him back the cows that belonged to him. Olaf told him to take his cows, if he could distinguish them; "but don't delay our march." The peasant had with him a large house dog, which he put in among the herd of cattle, in which many hundred head of beasts were driven together. The dog ran into the herd, and drove out exactly the number which the peasant had said he wanted; and all were marked with the same mark, which showed that the dog knew the right beasts, and was very sagacious. Olaf then asked the peasant if he would sell him the dog. "I would rather give him to you," said the peasant. Olaf immediately presented him with a gold ring in return, and promised him his friendship in future. This dog was called Vige, and was the very best of dogs, and Olaf owned him long afterwards.'

Back in Scandinavia, Vige proved a great help to Olaf in his pursuit of an enemy.

'When the king saw where Thorer Hjort, who was quicker on foot than any man, was running to, he ran after him with his dog Vige. The king said, "Vige! Vige! Catch the deer." Vige ran straight in upon him; on which Thorer halted, and the king threw a spear at him. Thorer struck with his sword at the dog, and gave him a great wound; but at the same moment the king's spear flew under Thorer's arm, and went through and through him, and came out at his otherside. There Thorer left his life; but Vige was carried to the ships.'

In another tale of the north, the Icelandic, *Saga of Burnt Njal*, dated to 1000 AD, Olaf, the son of an Irish princess, gives an Irish hound to his friend Gunnar Jarl, an Icelandic settler:

'Olaf said, "I will give thee three things of price, a gold ring, and a cloak which Moorkjartan the Erse king owned, and a hound
that was given me in Ireland; he is big, and no worse follower than a sturdy man. Besides, it is part of his nature that he has man's wit, and he will bay at every man whom he knows is thy foe,
but never at thy friends; he can see, too, in any man's face, whether he means thee well or ill, and he will lay down his life to be true to thee. This hound's name is Sam."

After that he spoke to the hound, "Now shalt thou follow
Gunnar, and do him all the service thou canst."

The hound went at once to Gunnar and laid himself down at his
feet.'

The qualities of being able to spot, 'the smiling assassin' and
being faithful unto death, recur time and again in the story of the
Irish greyhound. Gunnar's enemies plotted to kill him but were
always wary of his faithful, Irish hound:

"Then ye two shall sometime after make an attack on Gunnar,
but still ye must not seek him at home, for there is no
thinking of that while the hound is alive."

The plotters gathered in preparation for the attack:

'Mord said that they could not come on Gunnar unawares,
unless they seized the farmer who dwelt at the next homestead,
whose name was Thorkell, and made him go against his will
with them to lay hands on the hound Sam, and unless he went
before them to the homestead to do this.

Then they set out east for Lithend, but sent to fetch Thorkell.
They seized him and bound him, and gave him two choices –
one that they would slay him, or else he must lay hands on the
hound; but he chooses rather to save his life, and went with
them.

There was a beaten sunk road, between fences, above the
farmyard at Lithend, and there they halted with their band.
Master Thorkell went up to the homestead, and the tyke lay
on the top of the house, and he entices the dog away with him
into a deep hollow in the path. Just then the hound sees that

there are men before them, and he leaps on Thorkell and tears his belly open.

Aunund of Witchwood smote the hound on the head with his axe, so that the blade sunk into the brain. The hound gave such a great howl that they thought it passing strange, and he fell down dead.

Gunnar woke up in his hall and said, "Thou hast been sorely treated, Sam, my fosterling, and this warning is so meant that our two deaths will not be far apart."

Gunnar died making a heroic defence just like his noble hound. In the 1014, the Dalcassian soldiers who fought with Brian Boru against the Danes at Clontarf, are said to have been compared to,

'…the terrible, nimble wolfdogs of Ireland for strength and courage.'
(The Dalcassians were an Irish tribe headed by Brian Boru)

In February, 1035, we have the following mention in *The Annals of Ulster*, most probably of an Irish greyhound, dying in defence of his master:

'Cathal son of Amalgaid, King of Western Laigin, (Leinster), and his wife, i.e., the daughter of the son of Gilla Caemgein son of Cinaed, and his hound were killed at the same time by the son of Cellach son of Dúnchad.' *The Annals of the Four Masters* add, 'and by Aed son of Tuathal.'

Gerald de Barri, of Wales, gives us two stories from the 12th century of a dog's devotion to its master, the dogs in question possibly being Irish greyhounds.

'Cadwalladon, through inveterate malice, slew his brother Owen; a greyhound belonging to the aforesaid Owen, large, beautiful, and curiously spotted with a variety of colours, received seven wounds from arrows and lances in the defence of his master, and on his part did much injury to the enemy and assassins. When his wounds were healed, he was sent to King Henry II by William Earl of Gloucester, in testimony of so great and extraordinary a deed.'

The second story concerns the battle of Coleshill/Ewloe in 1157, between the Welsh, led by Prince Owain Gwynedd and the English, led by King Henry II, in Flintshire, north Wales, when the English had been defeated.

'In this wood of Coleshille a young Welshman was killed while passing through the King's army; the greyhound who accompanied him did not desert his master's corpse for eight days, though without food; but faithfully defended it from the attacks of dogs, wolves, and birds of prey, with a wonderful attachment: What son to his father? What Nisus to Euryalus? What Polynices to Tydeus? What Orestes to Pylades, would have shown such an affectionate regard? As a mark of favour to the dog, who was almost starved to death, the English, although bitter enemies to the Welsh, ordered the body, now nearly putrid, to be deposited in the ground with the accustomed offices of humanity.'

England's affairs became intertwined with Ireland's, when in 1168, Dermott Mac Murrough, the deposed King of Leinster, applied for help to King Henry II of England. He secured the services of Richard de Clare, 2nd Earl of Pembroke, better known as, Strongbow, promising him the succession and his daughter Eva's hand in marriage. Strongbow crossed over in 1170, retook Dublin and Waterford and married Eva.

In May 1171, Mac Murrough died and his old enemy, King Roderick of Connaught invaded his lands, Strongbow could but hold on to Dublin and soon afterwards returned to England to obtain help from Henry. Henry led a force across in October 1172, stayed six months and seems to have been acknowledged as overlord by Roderick.

From this point on we begin to hear much more about the Irish greyhound in specific references. John, son of Henry II, (younger brother of Richard I), and King of England from 1199 to 1216, gave orders on the 14th of May, 1201 at Portsmouth via his chamberlain, Hubert, to Henry Fitzwarin to find accommodation for his Irish hounds.

There is further reference to King John's association with the breed in the following communication:

'The King, &c., To The Baron, &c.

Pay to Henry de Neville 10 marks each year for four years for the wages of Odo and Richard, who have the charge of our wolfhounds, (luvereticos), and 40 shillings each year for their ponies, and 30 shillings each year for their livery.

As witness my hand at Lambeth, 29th day of April, in the 7th year, &c.

By G. Fitz-Peter'
AD 1206

Llywelyn II, 'Fawr or The Great', Prince of Wales, married Joan Lackland, King John's illegitimate daughter in 1201, and in 1210 it is said that the King gave Llywelyn the gift of an Irish greyhound, which he named Gelert.

Llywelyn lived near Snowdon and like most medieval monarchs was devoted to hunting and Gelert would always accompany his master on these trips. One morning however, the hound held back from accompanying his master, perhaps sensing an unseen danger, but I will let the poet take up the tale.

Beth Gelert; or the Grave of the Greyhound

The spearmen heard the bugle sound,
And cheerily smiled the morn;
And many a brach, and many a hound
Obeyed Llywelyn's horn.

And still he blew a louder blast,
And gave a lustier cheer,
"Come, Gelert, come, wert never last
Llywelyn's horn to hear."

"O where does faithful Gelert roam,
The flower of all his race;
So true, so brave – a lamb at home,
A lion in the chase?"

Twas only at Llywelyn's board
The faithful Gelert fed;
He watched, he served, he cheered his lord,
And sentinelled his bed.

In sooth he was a peerless hound,
The gift of Royal John;
But now no Gelert could be found,
And all the chase rode on.

And now, as o'er the rocks and dells
The gallant chidings rise,
All Snowdon's craggy chaos yells
The many mingled cries.

That day Llywelyn little loved
The chase of hart and hare;
And scant and small the booty proved,
For Gelert was not there.

Unpleased, Llywelyn homeward hied,
When near the portal seat,
His truant Gelert he espied,
Bounding his lord to greet.

But when he gained the castle door
Aghast the chieftain stood;
The hound all o'er was smeared with gore,
His lips his fangs ran blood.

Llywelyn gazed with fierce surprise;
Unused such looks to meet,
His favourite checked his joyful guise,
And crouched and licked his feet.

Onward in haste Llywelyn passed,
And on went Gelert too;
And still where'er his eyes he cast,
Fresh blood-gouts shocked his view.

Overturned his infant's bed he found,
With blood-stained cover rent;
And all around the walls and ground
With recent blood besprent.

He called his child – no voice replied –
He searched with terror wild;
Blood, blood he found on every side,
But nowhere found his child.

"Hell-hound! My child's by thee devoured,"
The frantic father cried;
And to the hilt his vengeful sword
He plunged in Gelert's side.

His suppliant looks, as prone he fell,
No pity could impart;
But still his Gelert's dying yell
Passed heavy o'er his heart.

Arous'd by Gelert's dying yell,
Some slumb'rer waken'd nigh:
What words the parent's joy could tell,
To hear his infant's cry!

Concealed beneath a tumbled heap
His hurried search had missed,
All glowing from his rosy sleep,
The cherub boy he kissed.

Nor scathe had he, nor harm, nor dread,
But, the same couch beneath,
Lay a gaunt wolf all torn and dead,
Tremendous still in death.

Ah, what was then Llywelyn's pain!
For now the truth was clear;
His gallant hound the wolf had slain,
To save Llywelyn's heir.

Vain, vain was all Llywelyn's woe;
"Best of thy kind, adieu!
The frantic blow, which laid thee low,
This heart shall ever rue."

And now a gallant tomb they raise,
With costly sculpture decked;
And marbles storied with his praise
Poor Gelert's bones protect.

There never could the spearman pass,
Or forester, unmoved;
There, oft the tear-besprinkled grass
Llywelyn's sorrow proved.

And there he hung his horn and spear,
And there, as evening fell,
In fancy's ear he oft would hear
Poor Gelert's dying yell.

And till great Snowdon's rocks grow old,
And cease the storm to brave,
The consecrated spot shall hold
The name of 'Gelert's grave'.

W.R. Spencer

The child in the tale must have been Dafyd ap Llywelyn, his only son by Joan and eventually his successor. This tragic story is thought to have been the reason for the old Welsh proverb:

'I am as sorry as the man that killed the greyhound.'

There is an interesting footnote to this story in that a couple, namely, Kathryn and Brian Pritchard Gibson, bought a farm in Wales, with a 17th century manor house, 'Pen y Bryn', in 1992. The house is sited on a hillside in Snowdonia and has always been known by the locals as, Tyr Llywelyn or Llywelyn's Tower. Being keen students of history and their appetites being whetted by tales from the locals, the Gibsons started researching their home and literally digging up the past. Although most of the house is 17th century, there is a tower at one end, which has been dated to 1211 and an old barn has turned out to have been a chapel from the same period. Further research has revealed that this is where Joan, the wife of Llywelyn Fawr lived and died. This, then, would be the most likely location for the events contained in, *The Grave of the Greyhound,* the location, the chronology and the fact that Llywelyn and his wife lived there all fits with the story.

In 1224, we hear of Hugh O'Connor, King of Connaught and Mac Branan his Steward of Hounds, who, as was usual in those days, was also head of the army.

'Longshanks', King Edward I, the, 'Hammer of the Scots', and indeed the Welsh, ordered Irish hounds in 1280 and I think it likely that he got what he sent for. We have a further record in that:

'William de Reynes formerly held two carucates, (240 acres), of land in Boyton, in the parish of Finchingfield, in the county of Essex, by the serjeantry of keeping for the King five wolfdogs (Canes Luporarios).'

Edward II appears to have kept up his predecessors' interest in the great hounds.

'In the 15 Edward II, Queenhull manor, Worcestershire, was held of the King by rendering yearly, 'unum canem de mota':

(one dog), and, in the preceding year of his reign, William Michell, of Middleton Lillebon, in Wiltshire, held land for keeping the King's wolfdogs.'

Edward III sent his huntsman, Reginald, to retrieve nineteen hounds from Irish lords on the 24th August 1335. No doubt they were part of a tribute paid to the English King, a tribute, which had most likely been ongoing since the time of Henry II.

'A huntsman, Reginald, goes to Ireland to get some, taking boys with him who receive a wage of three pence halfpenny a day. A halfpenny is allowed per day for each dog to get it food, and he obtained 19 of such dogs from various lords.'

A later envoy setting out for the same purpose was said to have been taken hostage by the Irish, what happened to him is not recorded.

From the 15th century Irish work, the *Book of Lismore*, we have mention that.

'...each of these hounds is as big as an ass.'

A story frequently connected with the Irish greyhound is, *The Dog of Montargis*. Now the dog in the story has been described as a greyhound and a wolfdog in different versions, so naturally the two became linked, but of course we cannot be certain the canine involved was an Irish greyhound.

The events of the story are said to have taken place in France in the year 1371, during the reign of Charles V, 'the Wise'. A squire of the King's house, Aubrie de Montdidier, was returning from court, (possibly the Chateau de Vincennes), to his home, passing through the forest of Bondi, when an envious rival named Richard Macaire, ambushed him and killed him without warning. Montdidier owned an Irish greyhound 'Dragon', by name, who had at the time in question been off hunting in the forest. When the dog returned and found his dead master it was said he nosed leaves around the body and then lay with it for three days, at the end of this period hunger made it rise and return to the court. Back at court, the greyhound chanced upon Macaire and attacked him, but was restrained by others from doing damage. The dog then took food from the table and returned to its master, attempting to feed him. For some time the dog issued back and forth from court to forest and every time it saw Macaire it flew into a rage and had to be restrained. News of this strange behaviour reached the King and so he had the greyhound followed, whereupon Montdidier's body was discovered and duly buried. King Charles now was suspicious of Macaire and so commanded that his court make a fuss of the faithful hound by stroking and walking him etc. Charles then commanded Macaire to offer the dog some flesh, but the reaction was as before, with the greyhound attempting to maul him. The King was now convinced of Macaire's guilt, but there was no witness save the greyhound, so he ordered a trial by combat. Macaire was given a two-handed staff to defend himself with and the trial took place on the Isle de la Cite in Paris before the King and his court. Macaire lunged at his opponent but the greyhound danced round him until he caught Macaire off balance and then darted in, knocking him to the ground and seized him by the throat.

'And the King commanded that the greyhound, the which had Macaire under him, should be taken up, and then made enquiry of the truth at Macaire, the which acknowledged he had slain Aubrey by treason, and therefore he was hanged and drawn.
Edmund de Langley'

The story was committed to posterity by a monument in basso

relievo, which was on display on the chimney-piece of the great hall in the Castle of Montargis; hence the dog and tale becoming known as, *The Dog of Montargis*.

There is another version of the story set in an earlier time which does not name the dog, makes no mention of Montargis, and is said to have taken place in 780, in the reign of Charlemagne. The details can vary a little depending on the source, but the story takes place much as follows.

'In the early hours of an autumn morning, a young gentleman in the court of Charlemagne, (Charles the Great), the King of the Franks, was awoken from his slumber by the sound of scratching and a strange and pitiful moaning emitting from outside his home. Summoned by curiosity, he opened the door to the Paris streets to find an emaciated but still massive greyhound waiting for him on his step. The animal, showed no signs of aggression, only sorrow, as it whimpered to signify its hunger. For his part, the man showed no sign of fear, for he instantly recognized the dog as belonging to his friend, Chevalier Aubrey de Montdidier, an archer in the King's guard, and knew it to be not only an exceedingly faithful creature, but surprisingly gentle for one with such a fearsome facade.

Recognizing the animal's hunger the man led it inside, where he fed it the remnants of yesterday's meal along with a bowlful of milk. As the famished dog devoured the meal, the man's thoughts returned to his friend. It had been days since he or anyone else had last seen Aubrey at a Sunday's mass, after which he had failed to keep any of his appointments. Worried, a few of his friends called upon him at his home but he wasn't to be found. And here was his faithful dog, nearly starved, with his master's whereabouts unknown.

The man was retrieved from his dark thoughts by a tug at his sleeve, the result of Aubrey's hound having taken a hold of his shirt between its teeth. Having gained the man's attention it released its grip and moved toward the door, indicating with a shallow bark that it wanted out. The man did as asked and the creature exited only to stop after a few steps to look back and see if he would follow. He did not. Eventually the animal wandered off into the darkness.

The man was haunted by the encounter and the next day he redoubled his efforts to find Aubrey, but no one had seen or heard word of him since that Sunday's mass. As for his dog, others had also encountered the animal, which had been making a ritual of appearing every three or four days at the homes of old acquaintances of his master, begging to be fed, only to disappear after its hunger was staved.

A few days later the dog again showed up at his doorstep, moaning pitifully. The man fed the creature, but this time when it left he followed dutifully behind, sending word to others by way of a young apprentice he encountered. These friends of Aubrey joined him in following the animal out of Paris along the road north that led deep into the tangled Forest of Bondi, a place with a foul reputation as a haunt for bandits and outlaws.

It was there in the dark forest that the dog's journey came to an end. Coming upon a great tree, it lay down at its trunk on a patch of recently disturbed earth and commenced to howl mournfully. The men knew instantly what had summoned the beast to this spot.

With their bare hands the men dug up the ground and soon unearthed Aubrey from his grave, a wound on his back revealing where the assassin had laid him low. To all present it was readily apparent what had happened: their friend Aubrey, somehow, had been led out to this forsaken location, only to be attacked and buried where none but his hound would know. The animal, so faithful and loyal, had remained to stand watch over his grave for all these days, only leaving when compelled by hunger, and even then returning as soon as possible to continue its lonely vigil.

The men returned the body to Paris, where it was given a proper burial. The dog stayed beside his master until he was interred, after which a friend of Aubrey's took the dog as his own, or, more accurately, the dog took the man as his own. The mystery of Chevalier Montdidier's disappearance had been solved, but the identity of his killer remained unknown.

That is until one day, as Aubrey's friend strolled with his dog through the city streets, it suddenly sprang in front of him and growled menacingly at the crowd before them. As the man tried to determine what about the crowd agitated the beast so greatly, it charged into the mass of people to lunge at a chevalier. Luckily, the man had raised his arm in time to deflect the animal and save his throat from being ripped out. With the help of two other passers-by, they were able to fend off the animal by beating it and wrestling it away from its would-be victim. With Aubrey's hound restrained, the man took the opportunity to flee as the dog frothed and glared at him with baleful eyes. That the dog would display such aggressive behaviour was, to say the least, very surprising, for he had always been gentle and never known to attack any man. Now, here it had tried to maul this stranger, but only him, as Aubrey's friend noted, for it did no harm to anyone else present, even those that had themselves attacked the animal.

At first the man thought nothing of the matter, but over the passing days as he mentioned the story to friends, he was shocked to learn that this man, one Chevalier Macaire, had been no stranger, but had served alongside Montdidier in the King's guard. Furthermore, he and Aubrey had been bitter rivals. Suspicions now entered the man's mind as to why the hound despised this Macaire so strongly.

Less than a week later these suspicions were only reinforced when, during a stroll through a garden with Montdidier's hound in tow behind him, Macaire came into view. Immediately the dog went on the attack, Macaire only being saved when a group of bystanders delayed the animal long enough to allow him to escape through the garden gates, which he closed keeping the frothing animal at bay.

Word of these incidents soon reached King Charles the Great. Since both the victim and the suspect had been gentlemen of the court, it fell under the King's authority, and interest, to judge such a strange case. To test the veracity of these wild claims he summoned the hound, who appeared before the King displaying its usual friendly demeanour to all present. He then had a large group of attendants brought into the room amongst which Macaire had been hid. The dog, who had peacefully ignored all the day's activities, suddenly sprang up as he caught the hated Macaire's scent. It then charged through the crowd towards him and was only denied its prey by the combined efforts of several men who forcibly removed the animal. The King, having witnessed the hound's strange behaviour firsthand, now questioned Macaire intently, but he denied any involvement in the death of Aubrey de Montdidier.

Unable to decide in either party's favour based on such

circumstantial evidence, the King ordered that the case be judged by God's favour, a trial by combat, with innocence or guilt to be determined on the Ile de la Cité, an island on the Seine that would eventually be the location of the Notre Dame de Paris, Cathedral.

On the day of combat, the whole of the court was in attendance to witness this duel between man and dog. The area of fighting had been roped off; stands had been constructed for the King and other nobles to gain a better view. Macaire was given a thick baton for his defence, while the dog, which was expected to fight with his natural weapons, was given a barrel in which he could retreat. Thus evenly armed the two were brought onto the lists and the signal was given to commence.

Macaire stood his ground as the hound rushed him, only to halt just short of the baton's striking range. There, always outside of his reach, the animal darted swiftly to the right and left, dodging Macaire's heavy blows until finally the Chevalier tired and dropped his guard. An instant was all the dog needed as it immediately pounced upon Macaire, clamping its jaws around his throat. Macaire, only saved by his coat's collar, fought desperately to get the dog off him. When that proved impossible, he screamed for mercy. The crowd shouted back at him "God's judgements are the best," and demanded that he confess the crime before ending the trial. Macaire swore he would do so and the attendants immediately pulled the now raging beast off him.

Macaire did as promised detailing how, under the pretence of a hunting trip, he had led Aubrey into the Forest of Bondi. There, after Aubrey's hound had taken off after a stag injured by its master's arrow, Macaire cowardly stabbed his hated rival in the back with his spear. He then buried the body and rode off just as the dog was returning from his hunt.

With God having passed judgement (along with Macaire's confession) the assassin was ordered to climb the scaffold a week later. With the execution of Macaire, Aubrey Montdidier's most faithful companion had avenged the murder of his master.'

Most of these details come from Jean de la Traille's, *Discours Notable Des Duels*, of 1607.

The following are details I came across of an old square dance tune during my researches:

'**FOREST OF BONDI** See 'Forest de Bondi'. English? Country Dance (2/4 time). D Major. Standard. AABB. The tune, titled after a forest near Paris, France, has a long history in New England. It appears in a musician's manuscript copybook called, *'The Read Manuscript'*, from New Haven, Connecticut, dated 1798. As *'Forest de BondiSquare Dance'*, the tune appears in the repertoire list of Maine fiddler, Mellie Dunham (Bronner, 1987). The elderly Dunham was Henry Ford's champion fiddler in the late 1920s. Howe (c. 1867) prints instructions for a contra-dance to the tune.

I believe the title refers to a once well-known tale of canine attachment that is said to have occurred during the reign of Charles V.'

Although the dog is referred to simply as a greyhound, two key words lead me to believe the writer was referring to an Irish greyhound, namely, it was described as massive and fearsome. Words that just would not be used to describe an ordinary greyhound.

Similar faithful hounds are mentioned by Plutarch in his, *De Sollertia Animalium* (*Moralia*). (On the intelligence of animals).

'There was a Roman named Calvus slain in the Civil Wars, but no one was able to cut off his head until they encircled and stabbed to death the dog who guarded his master and defended him. And King Pyrrhus on a journey chanced upon a dog guarding the body of a murdered man; in answer to his questions he was told that the dog had remained there without eating for three days and refused to leave. Pyrrhus gave orders for the corpse to be buried and the dog cared for and brought along in his train. A few days later there was an inspection of the soldiers, who marched in front of the King seated on his throne, while the dog lay quietly by his side. But when it saw its master's murderers filing past, it rushed at them with furious barking and, as it voiced its accusation, turned to look at the King so that not only he, but everyone present, became suspicious of the men. They were at once arrested and when put to the question, with the help of some bits of external evidence as well, they confessed the murder and were punished.'

In *The Annals of Ulster*, there is an entry in the year 1409, recording the following occurrence.

'The leg of Richard Burke was broken by a greyhound that rushed against him, while running at full speed; and he died in consequence.'

There is another legend associated with the Irish greyhound, and that is the story of, 'The Dog Leap', in Limavady, County Derry. It is supposed to have occurred sometime in the Middle Ages and proceeds as follows.

The O'Cahans were the most dominant family in the region and controlled an area stretching from the river Bann in the east to

Lough Foyle in the west and were vassals to the powerful O'Neills. Their headquarters and main castle was at Dungiven but they had another castle beside the river Roe near present day Limavady. The story has it that a rival clan attacked the castle at Limavady and was in danger of overwhelming the garrison. Inside the castle a message requesting immediate reinforcement was written on a piece of vellum and attached to the collar of an Irish greyhound which had often made the trip between the two castles with its master.

The dog on being ejected from the castle, raced past the enemy, dodging spears and stones thrown in its direction and headed south toward Dungiven, along the bank of the river Roe. A few of the enemy mounted horses and took off in pursuit hoping to intercept the dog before it reached its destination. After some time the enemy began bearing down on the dog, thrusting with their spears. The dog looked to his left and made a desperate leap from a high ledge over the river and landed safely on the opposite bank below. His pursuers could only look on in frustration as the dog made its way onward to Dungiven to deliver his message. Reinforcements were hastily despatched and the castle was saved.

Although there is little but a few stones marking the site of Limavady castle today, a sculpture of a leaping dog has been installed at 'The Dog Leap', in Roe Valley Country Park to commemorate the story.

In 1505, the Portuguese built a fort at Sofala in what is now Mozambique, which was soon afterwards attacked by a substantial local force. Details of the defence are given in, *Decadas da Asia, (Decades of Asia)*, by Joao de Barros.

'…there were only thirty-five men in the fortress who could
bear arms and the others were in such a state that it took
five or six of them to draw a crossbow, and the best men at
arms, Pedro d'Anaya had in the fortress at that time, and that
guarded it both night and day, were two large greyhounds,

56

which the Kaffirs feared more than the fury of the lances and
swords of our men, for though they struck with a good will
they had no strength in their arms to hurt them. It would
seem that through these two animals that God wished to
show a part of the favour which he granted us against these
barbarians, for the dogs had a great hatred of those without,
but towards the Moors within the fortress they were as tame as
towards any of the Portuguese.'

Were these Irish greyhounds? It is a possibility, certainly they must
have been more formidable than the ordinary run of the mill
greyhound.

In 1525, the Earl of Kildare brought a charge against the Earl
of Ormond that:

'...he exacted coyne and livery throughout Tipperary and
Kilkenny for his sundry hunts, that is to say, twenty-four
persons with sixty greyhounds and hounds for deer-hunting;
another number of men and dogs for to hunt the hare, and a
third number to hunt the martin.'

In 1535, Thomas Cromwell, later to become the first
Earl of Essex, received a brace of Irish greyhounds from Philip
Roche, a merchant of Kinsale, county Cork with the following
communication:

'Your mastership shall understand that I have sent with your
servant, Davy Shihan, to be presented to your mastership,
two falcons and three merlins, and a sparrow hawk, two
greyhounds, and I trust before long to have a goshawk to send
to your mastership, and for any hawks or greyhounds that
your mastership shall lack, write to me and I will purvey to
your mastership by God's grace.'

We even have evidence that the Irish greyhound made it to the new world, in the company of one, Hernando de Soto, a Spanish conquistador. *The De Soto Chronicles. The Expedition of Hernando de Soto to North America in 1539-1543. Vol II*, edited by Clayton, Knight and Moore, contains the following records of de Soto's Irish greyhound Bruto.

'The greyhound, which happened to be nearby, hearing the shout the Indians gave and seeing them run, followed them. As if he had human understanding, he passed by the first whom he overtook and also the second and the third, until reaching the fourth, who was running ahead. Seizing him by the shoulder, he threw him down and held him on the ground. Meanwhile the Indian who was nearest came up; as the dog saw that he was passing by, he loosed the first one and caught the one who was passing, and having thrown him down, he grasped the third, who was now passing by, and having done the same with him as with the first two, he went at the fourth, who now came up. Throwing him to the ground, he returned to the others and ran between them with such dexterity and skill, leaping at the one who was down and grasping and pulling down him who raised up, and threatening them with loud barks at the same time that he seized them, that he confused and held them until the Spaniards came up to their assistance. They took the four Indians and returned with them to the camp. Taking each one separately, they questioned them as to why they had fled, so without occasion, fearing that this might be a countersign for some treachery that they had plotted. All four replied as one person that they had done it for no reason at all except a vain fancy that seized them, it appearing to them that it would be a great exploit and proof of gallantry and agility if they should escape from the midst of the Castilians in that manner. They thought to boast of this brave exploit later among the Indians, because of its being in their opinion a great victory, of which they had been deprived by the hound Bruto, for so the dog was named.

At this point Juan Coles, having recounted some of the things we have told, tells of another particular exploit of the hound Bruto. He says that on another river, before coming to Ocali, some Indians and Spaniards being on its bank talking together peacefully, one daring Indian, there being many such, gave a Castilian a hard blow with his bow, for no reason whatever, and then jumped into the water, and all his people followed him. He says that the hound, which was nearby, seeing what had happened, jumped in after them, and although he overtook other Indians, he says that he did not seize any of them until he came to the one who struck the blow, and grasping him, he tore him to pieces in the water.

For these attacks and for others that Bruto had made upon them while guarding the army at night, so that no enemy Indian approached it whom he did not immediately destroy, the Indians avenged themselves by killing him as has been told.'

Bruto's end was an honourable one, caused by his own reckless courage.

'At the shout the Indians raised on shooting their arrows, a greyhound, which one of the governor's pages was leading by the collar, jumped and knocked down the page, dragging him on the ground. He gave a leap and threw himself into the water, and however much the Spaniards might call to him, he would not come back. Seeing the dog swimming, the Indians shot at him so skilfully that they placed more than fifty arrows in his head and shoulders, which were exposed. With all this the dog was able to come out on the bank, but on leaving the water he at once fell dead. This grieved the governor and all his people very much, because he was an extremely fine animal and much needed in the conquest, during which, in the short time that it had lasted, he had made forays that caused no little wonder against the Indian enemies, both by day and by night...'

Bruto was truly a formidable and sagacious animal, traits frequently made mention of by old writers describing the Irish greyhound.

In 1545, King Henry VIII received a request from the Duke of Alberkyrk, a member of his privy council, on behalf of the Marquis Desarrya, a Spanish nobleman and his son:

'...that it might please his Majesty to grant to the said Marquis and his son, and the longer liver of them yearly, out of Ireland two goshawks and four greyhounds,'

Henry agreed and commanded the Irish Lord Deputy, Sir Anthony Sentleger, to order the delivery of the hawks and hounds and to charge the cost to the Treasury.

In 1548, during the reign of Edward VI, Lord Deputy Bellingham, wrote to one James Hancock, merchant and later Mayor of Dublin, reproaching him for:

'...his wilful obstinacy, by which His Majesty was in danger of being disappointed as to certain dogs for a nobleman in Spain, which he, the Deputy, had promised.'

Whether or not this was a continuation of the grant awarded by Henry VIII, I do not know, but it seems likely.

In November 1562, as we learn from the State Papers relating to Ireland, the Irish chieftain, Shane O'Neill, forwarded to Queen Elizabeth, through her favourite, Robert Dudley, Earl of Leicester, a present of two horses, two hawks, and two Irish wolfdogs.

Edmund Campion, a brilliant Elizabethan scholar wrote, *A History of Ireland*, around 1571, at Turvey, near Dublin and said:

'The Irish are not without wolves and greyhounds to hunt them, bigger of bone and limme than a colt.'

Richard Stanihurst, in his, *Description of Ireland*, published by Raphael Holinshed in, *Chronicles of England, Scotland and Ireland*, in 1577 writes:

'They are not without wolves, and greyhounds to hunt them, bigger of bone and limb than a colt.'

Evidently copying the earlier work by Campion.

In 1585, Sir John Perrott, Lord Deputy of Ireland and said to be an illegitimate son of Henry VIII, sent a brace of Irish greyhounds to Sir Francis Walsingham, Elizabeth I's spymaster.

'...a brace of good wolfdogs, one black, one white.'

William Camden, writing around 1586, said in his, *Britannia*:

'The Irish wolfhound is similar in shape to a greyhound, bigger than a mastiff, and tractable as a spaniel.'

In 1587, one Emmery de Lew, wrote to Lord Willoughby requesting the Irish greyhound (levrier d' Irlande), which he had promised him.

Sir Brian O'Rourke, Lord of West Breifne, who had been fighting against the English forces in Ireland, went to Glasgow in

1591, most likely to solicit help from King James VI of Scotland, later to become James I of England. O'Rourke took with him four Irish greyhounds and six hobbies as a gift for the King, unfortunately for him Elizabeth had already been in communication with James about his visit, and as a result he was seized and transported to London, where he was convicted of treason and hanged, drawn and quartered.

Grace O'Malley, the famous 'Pirate Queen' of Mayo, sailed to London in 1593 for a personal meeting with Queen Elizabeth I at Richmond Palace, to air grievances against Sir Richard Bingham. The English governor of Connaught who had been waging a vendetta against her and her clan. It is said she took along four Irish greyhounds as part of her retinue, most likely as a gift for the queen. Unlike O'Rourke, Grace was successful in her suit, probably because Elizabeth saw something of herself in the Pirate Queen and respected another strong woman in a man's world.

The Irish greyhound's reputation had spread across Europe so much so, that Henry the Great, King of France wrote a letter on the 29th December 1595 to the Earl of Essex, Queen Elizabeth's new favourite, requesting a pair of them:

'To the other obligations that I am under to you I must add this one, that you procure for me a greyhound of Ireland and a bitch of the same race, in order that I may keep up the breed. You know how much I love the chase, and this gift will enable me to while away time, and sometimes to capture wild boars, and essay, if the goodness of these dogs is equal to the reputation that they have. Believe me, I will be fond of them, and will keep them for your sake; in return for this present you can command my service in any way you wish.'

It says a great deal about the value of these dogs, when a gift of them could win great favour from a personage as important as the King of France, one of the most powerful rulers in Europe.

In May of 1596, Guicciardini, (an agent of Essex), in a letter to him added as a postscript:

'If you do determine to present the Duke (of Tuscany) with anything from thence, there will be nothing so acceptable unto him as some dogs of that country of Ireland that are fair and fierce for the wild boar.'

Lope de Vega, considered the Spanish Shakespeare, wrote a sonnet about the Irish greyhound about the year 1596, in which he describes one being barked at by a pack of street dogs:

What Lofty Minds Ought To Do When People Murmur Against Them

An Irish greyhound of beauteous build,
Bay-coloured, dark-striped from head to haunch,
His collar worked in bronze with buff breast-piece
Was passing by the sideway of a street.
Out sallied pell-mell an army barking at him,
A pack of curs, black, red and white,
As from a village in fury they tear away
To pursue the wolf over hill and dale;
And as, the writers say, the tranquil triform Moon,
That silver orb on the celestial satin,
Sets all the dogs of the mountain mad.
This highborn greyhound, without heeding them,
Lifted his leg, wet the projecting angle of the wall,
And through the midst of them went on quite at his ease.

In 1600, Dr Peter Lombard, Primate of Armagh, stated that the finest hunting dogs in Europe were produced in Ireland:

'In Ireland are bred the fairest and best hunting dogs of
all Europe, as it is esteemed, and they are of various kinds.
There are dogs that hunt by scent, water-dogs that pursue
water-fowl; others there are which partly are in form and size
common to other regions, and hunt hares, rabbits, and foxes;
and partly are much larger and most powerful in capturing
stags, boars and wolves.'

Also in 1600, Noel de Carron, writing to Sir Robert Cecil,
informs him that he has made known to Maurice Prince of
Orange, that Cecil is sending three dogs from Ireland to him.

Fynes Moryson, Secretary to Baron Mountjoy, Lord Deputy
from 1600 to 1603 said:

'The men and greyhounds of Ireland are of great stature...
The destruction of wolves being neglected by the inhabitants,
being oppressed with greater mischiefs, they are so much
grown in number as sometimes in winter nights they will
come to prey in villages and the suburbs of cities.'

Sir Arthur Chichester, Lord Deputy of Ireland from 1604 to
1614, wrote to Viscount Cranbourne, (William Cecil), the son of
Lord Salisbury, (Robert Cecil), in 1605:

'I endeavour my best to get fair dogs for you, of which the
country is very scarce, the Lord Deputy, (his predecessor,
Carew), having sent so many as he can get already into
England. Seeing you desire them, I will henceforth breed some
for you, and in the meantime send such as I can get.'
That same year Chichester sent to Salisbury:

'...some dogs and a bitch great with whelps; they are good and
the fairest that this kingdom affords.'

In a further letter Chichester wrote that he had sent some more Irish greyhounds but they had been lost at sea when the ship foundered.

The following year he sent:

'...the fairest dogs in this kingdom, thinking you would have occasion to dispose of them upon the coming of the King of Denmark.' (King Christian IV)

The Cecils obtained around thirty over a five-year period. Lord Willoughby was also said to have acquired Irish dogs, as has already been seen from Emmery de Lew's request of 1587.

In Edward Topsell's, *Historie of four-footed Beasts*, of 1607, he refers to large dogs called, 'Auges', brought from Ireland to France to be used as pack-leaders for hunting bears, wolves and wild boars, being equipped with broad, badger skin collars and being partly covered with 'thick clouts' for protection. These 'Auges' could only have been Irish greyhounds.

In 1608, we find that Irish wolfhounds were sent from Ireland by Captain Esmond of Duncannon, in Wexford, to Gilbert Talbot, 7th Earl of Shrewsbury.

In 1611, the following were the Heads of a Bill in the Dublin Parliament:

'An Act for killing wolves, touching the days of hunting, the people that are to attend, who will be their director; an inhibition not to use any arms; the Lord Deputy or Principal Governor to prohibit such hunting, if he suspect that such assemblies by wolf-hunting may prove inconvenient.'

In 1612, King James I granted a patent to one of his Irish subjects, Thomas Pott, Master of the Hunt, to keep twelve couples of wolfdogs in each county to protect the farmers' flocks from the ravages of wolves.

'In January, 1612, he received 153*l.* 12*s.* 5*d.,* for keeping twenty-four Irish dogs, and for the diet and entertainment of two servants to look to them, by direction of the late Prince Henry. He also had 50*l.,* for hunting them with Prince Henry of Nassau.'

(Prince Henry was the eldest son of James I and died in his eighteenth year).

R. Knolles, in his, *Turkish History*, published in 1687, records in a section dealing with Sultan Achmet I (r.1603-1617), that a parade in Constantinople included;

'Fifty Janizaries on foot, every one leading dogs in leashes, mastiffs or Irish grey-hounds, the goodliest of all were those the French Ambassador had presented unto the Sultan.'

The following is a story taken from the, *Dublin University Magazine Volume LVI*, of 1860. It encapsulates the very essence of the Irish greyhound, courage, antipathy to the wolf, loyalty, intelligence, nobility and that mysterious, almost supernatural element to its character, which led to so many tales being woven around the breed that the dog itself became legendary. I have reproduced it verbatim, as I found it thoroughly enjoyable and all the more enthralling because it happened within fifteen miles of where I sit!

'There is scarcely an old castle in the land that has not connected with it some marvellous tale or legend; and Antrim Castle is no exception. For more than a century, the traveller passing through the town of Antrim might have seen on the top of a turret of the castle, the figure, large as life, in solid stone, of one of that notable, but now extinct, race of animals, the Irish wolf-dog. The natives had an undefinable dread of it, and called the castle after it in Irish, as Anglicised, "the ugly Sassenach dog." The settlers too, especially those of the Scottish race, who retained many of the old superstitions of their country about, "witches and warlocks," and the like, felt no little awe of it. There was a mystery about the animal, and the way it came there, which they could not fathom. And as day by day, that dark impassive object met their view, with outstretched neck, bent on a "look out" towards Lough Neagh, they associated with it something of the supernatural; and they had good cause. The legend runs thus: Marian Langford, "the Lady Marian," the fair young wife of Sir Hugh Clotworthy, after the first few months of fondest endearment were over, began to feel that the bawn and the great court-yard, (for the castle was not then erected), made but a dreary abode. She missed in that interminable and solitary wood, the gaieties of the "rock," her early companions, and the old familiar scenes by Island Magee, the Green Isle, and Lough Morne. Sir Hugh himself was frequently absent on the dangerous services which his position imposed. On these occasions, to dispel the feeling of loneliness that oft-times came over her, she would wander forth from the bawn, by the great north gate, and direct her footsteps on the green banks of the river, to follow its meanderings in the woods, and in the hot summer's day, enjoy the cool and refreshing shade of that long arched bower. The wide-spreading branches of the forest trees stretching out from bank to bank, formed an ever-waving canopy of the richest foliage. Peopled as it was with innumerable feathered songsters, their sweet notes, joined to the murmurings of the waters, gave forth delicious music. Thus, shaded in a subdued light, with stray sunbeams glittering through the trees, a solemn stillness reigning throughout and the air impregnated with the fragrance of wild flowers, there could not be found in any clime a scene of higher beauty. One day she prolonged her accustomed walk until she reached the shores of Lough Neagh. Standing on the sandy beach, in front of a thicket, she viewed, with pleasurable emotion, the eddies and spray of the rushing waters as they foamed and bounded into the lake from a bar of sand which then crossed the mouth of the river. She was charmed also with the scenery of the lovely estuary of Antrim Bay, which lay before her view, enriched by dense woods that crept to the water's edge, overtopped on the opposite side by the lofty towers and battlements of Shane's Castle, the house of O' Neill, then standing in all its feudal grandeur, not as now, a venerable and ivy-clad ruin. She had not been long occupied thus when she heard a sharp growl from behind. Startled and alarmed she turned round, when, horror-struck, she beheld, a huge wolf, with distended jaws and eyes of fire, in the act of springing on her from the thicket. Uttering a scream of terror she fell to the ground. Her weakness saved her life, for the wolf missing his deadly spring, fell and rolled beyond her. Almost instantaneously another roar was heard, still louder than the first, and a second animal swept with lightning speed across her and seized the wolf. In the fearful noise and conflict of two ferocious animals fighting and tearing each other over her prostrate form she swooned. How long she remained insensible she never knew; but on regaining consciousness, she saw the wolf stretched on the bank, at some distance, mangled and dead; and lying by her side, licking her hand, and looking up wistfully into her face, with his large, trustful, mild, eyes, an Irish wolf-dog, panting and wounded. The noble animal had saved her life, and killed his natural enemy. The Lady Marian, with gratitude, and a woman's tenderness, had the suffering animal conveyed to the bawn, and tended with care. Her own fair hands dressed his wounds; and many a time in her walks she was accompanied by her dumb guardian friend, limping by her side. One day, shortly after he had recovered, the noble animal disappeared in the direction of Masserene Abbey, to the grief of his newly-found and tender mistress. Some considerable time elapsed. The castle was raised, and the incident of the wolf and the Irish wolf-dog was forgotten by all but the Lady Marian, whose gentle heart was touched by the devotion of the noble animal. One of those sudden, squally, storms from the lough, which are so frequent in that district, came on at the close of a dreary winter's day. The waves of the river ran unusually high, and were lashed with fury against the walls, whilst the forked lightning shot to and fro, like barbed spears of fire. Night suddenly descended, the lightning ceased, and the fitful sheets of flame and flashes of dazzling light which they produced were succeeded by an unbroken and impenetrable darkness. High over the wind, as it came in its headlong course roaring and crushing through the woods, the deep baying of a wolf-dog was heard. Round and round the walls of the castle it sounded in warning tones. Startled at an incident so unusual, the warders, by the direction of Sir Hugh (the Lady Marian exclaiming it was "the voice" of her "beloved Irish wolf-dog") sprang upon the mound. Hastily lighting up their turf and bogwood beacon-fire and pitch bog-fir torches, they saw by the glare of the light a dark mass of the Irish enemy, armed with matchlock, pike, and skein, and bearing some rude scaling ladders. A round shot from 'Roaring Tatty', the long gun of the mound, and a sharp fusillade from the bastions in their flank, rapidly dispersed the foe, and the castle and its inmates were released from danger. But what of the wolf-dog? Before the enemy left, a howling cry of pain was heard, accompanied by a few shots. During the night the storm continued as fiercely as ever, and the wail of the banshee was borne on the wind, moaning and sobbing by the river and the lough. One piercing screech towards the break of day, a last, concentrated, expiring gush of anguish it seemed to be, rose high above the storm, and then all was hushed and still. The wind abated, and soughed only occasionally through the trees, and the rain ceased to patter on the windows. In the grey dawn of the morning, as the warders went forth upon their round of inspection, they found, amidst fallen trees, and leaves, and broken branches, a stream of blood at the grand entrance gate, and some flattened musket balls by the wall side. But, most singular of all, on looking up towards the roof of the castle, they beheld, standing upon the highest turret, the wolf-dog himself, perfect in every limb, as he had left the Lady Marian some time before, but transformed into solid stone.

Such is the legend of the wolf-dog of Antrim Castle. But an old hard-headed unbeliever, Jacob Morgan by name, who had sailed round the world with Drake, used to dispute it roundly, and maintain – the old unromantic rogue – that all the story was true but the banshee and the turning of the dog into stone. The Lady Marian, he said, was saved from the wolf by the dog, who afterwards alarmed the garrison. The Irish in their fury shot the animal, which was of a superior and sagacious breed, kept by the monks of Massarine Abbey; and Sir Hugh, to gratify his lady, and leave a memorial of the event, had a figure of the dog cut in stone by a foreigner, "lying past him." Taking advantage of the storm he had it privately conveyed through a trap in the roof, and placed on the tower, to frighten the Irish. But no one minded Morgan, the old sinner; and the legend is believed in its integrity, and told at the hearthstone on the winter night, in all Massarine and Killead.

In after years when alterations were made on the roof of the Castle, and the front square towers were changed for columns, the wolf-dog was taken down, and placed close by the grand entrance gate, where the stream of blood and flattened musket balls were found on the morning after the storm and attack on the Castle. There he stands at this moment, a most interesting object, upon an angle of the southern bastion, now a terrace garden, and looks as if he were still the guardian sentinel of the park and castle. There is a prevalent tradition in the neighbourhood, that the extinction of the race of the fair Lady Marion Clotworthy, daughter of the stout old planter, Sir Roger Langford of Muckamore, need not be apprehended so long as her faithful Irish wolf-dog keeps watch and ward over her children there.'

A memorable tale I think you will agree, and although the castle is gone, the original motte and indeed the sculpture of the wolfdog still remains on display in Antrim Castle gardens. Sir Hugh, who was High Sheriff of Antrim, married Lady Marion in 1607, and the events recorded here are thought to have occurred around 1612.

Sir Thomas Roe, Ambassador to the Court of the Great Mogul Emperor of India, Jahangir, from December 23rd 1615, to the end of 1618, recorded the following request from said Emperor in 1617:

The Massarene Hound. Circa 1612. Photo by author.

Headshot of The Massarene Hound. Photo by author.

'I desire you to help me to a horse of the greatest size, and a male and female mastiff and the tall Irish greyhounds and such other dogs as hunt in your lands. If you will promise me this I will give you the word of a king that I will fully recompense you and grant you all your desires.' 'I answered,' said Sir Thomas, 'I would promise to provide them, but could not warrant their lives; and if they died on the way, only for my discharge their skins and bones should be preserved. He gave extraordinary bows, laid his hand on his heart; such kind gestures, as all men will witness, he never used to any man, nor such familiarity nor freedom nor profession of love.'

Cont'd:

'...must needs help him to one of our large horses, to a brace of Irish greyhounds, dog and bitch, and other dogs of all sorts, for game: which if I would procure him, he protested on the word of a Prince he would gratify me, and grant me more privileges than I should think of asking.'

An earlier shipment of dogs carried in Captain Benjamin Joseph's fleet, which also contained Roe's Chaplain, the Rev. Edward Terry, arrived at Surat in September 1615 after an eventful, and for the dogs, unfortunate voyage. No Irish greyhounds surviving the voyage, according to the Reverend Terry.

'In the year I went to India the merchants here, (as from the King of England, in whose name they sent all their presents), amongst many other things, sent the Mogul some great English mastiffs and some large Irish greyhounds, in all to the number of eight, dispersed in our several ships. One of these high-spirited mastiffs, upon a day seeing a great shoal of porpoises mounting up above the waves, and coming towards the ship wherein he was, leaped overboard to encounter them, wherein the fierce creature was irrevocably lost, the ship then having such a gale of wind that she could not suddenly slack her course.

Another, one of the great Irish greyhounds, had his head shot off in our sight. The mange was the destruction of four more of them. Only two of the mastiffs came alive to East India, and they were carried up, each in a little cart when I went up to the Ambassador (at Agra) that he might present them to the Mogul.'

From, *The Englishman in India*, by Charles Raikes, formerly Commissioner of Lahore, published in 1867, we find that the Irish greyhound lost its head during a sea battle with a Portuguese carrack from Goa, (probably cannon fire), a battle which also claimed the life of Captain Joseph.

Jahangir had previously been extremely pleased by the gift of a mastiff, as we can learn from the correspondence of Thomas Keridge, who was based in Ajmere, back to the British East India Company.

'Mr. Edwardes presented the king a mastife, and speaking of the dog's courage the king caused a younge leopard to be brought, to make tryall, wherewith the dog so pincht thatt (after) few houres life the leopard dyed; since, the king of Persia with a present sent hither haulfe a dozen dogges, the king caused boares to be brought to fight with them putting 2 or 3 dogs to a boare yett none of them seased and remembringe his owne dog sentt for him, who presently fastened on the boare, so disgraced the Persian dogs whereby the king was exceedingly pleased. 2 or 3 fierce mastyfes a couple of Irishe grayhoundes and a couple of well-bred water spanyells would give him greate content.'

Lady Alathea Howard, wife of the 2nd Earl of Arundel and daughter of Gilbert Talbot, was painted with Sir Dudley Carleton and an Irish greyhound by Peter Paul Rubens in 1620.

About the year 1623, Pott had a warrant to take:

'Six horses, a wagon with four horses for it, 20 couple of hounds, and 6 Irish greyhounds, as a present to the French King; as well as 6 horses for his own use.'

(The French king in question being Louis XIII).

On the 23rd of August 1623, the Irish Lord Deputy, Henry Cary, Viscount Falkland, wrote to Richard Boyle, the first Earl of Cork:

'I have lately received letters from my Lord Duke of Buckingham and others of my noble friends who have entreated me to send them some greyhound dogs and bitches out of this kingdom, of the largest sort, which I perceive they intend to present unto divers princes and other noble persons. And, if you can possibly, let them be white, which is the colour most in request here. Expecting your answer by the bearer, I commit you to the protection of the Almighty, and am your Lordship's attached friend – Falkland.'

Randle Cotgrave published a French-English Dictionary in the year 1632 with the following reference to the Irish greyhound:

'Levrier d' attaché – An Irish greyhound, a great greyhound.'

Thomas Wentworth, 1st Earl of Strafford and Lord Deputy of Ireland from 1632 to 1640, had his portrait painted with an Irish greyhound in 1633 and again in 1639 by no lesser an artist than Van Dyck.

From Richard Parr's, *Life of Ussher*, we learn that in 1641.

'On the publication of Ussher's work, '*De Primordiis Ecclesiarum Britannicarum*', Richelieu, (Cardinal), sent the author a gold medal and a complimentary letter; upon which Ussher presented the Cardinal with Irish greyhounds.'

Giovanni Battista Rinuccini, Papal Nuncio to Ireland from 1645 to 1649, writes of an Irish greyhound given to him in 1646, describing it as:

'...a most noble mollossus, very well able to overcome wolves and stags in fleetness, fighting and power; an animal, which by his majesty, great size, the marvellous variegation of his colour, and the proportion of his limbs, is so valuable as to be a gift fit to be presented to any emperor in the world.'

This was an Irish greyhound, which had been left behind by the Marquis of Ormond in his flight from Kilkenny on the 19th September 1646. The Nuncio returned with the dog to Italy and presented it to the Grand Duke of Tuscany, Fernando II de Medici, (r.1621-1670).

The lucrative export market for the Irish greyhound, together with those disaffected nobles going into exile with their dogs, led to the following declaration of 1652 by Oliver Cromwell:

DECLARATION AGAINST TRANSPORTING WOLFE DOGGES

'Forasmuch as we are credibly informed that wolves doe much increase and destroy many cattle in several partes of this dominion, and that some of the enemie's party who have laid down arms, and have liberty to get beyond the sea, and others, do attempt to carry away several such great dogges, as are commonly called wolfe dogges, whereby the breed of them, which are useful for destroying of wolves would, (if not prevented), speedily decay. These are therefore to prohibit all persons whatsoever from exporting any of the said dogges out of this dominion, and searchers and other officers of the customs, in the several partes and creekes of this dominion, are hereby strictly required to seize and make stop of all such dogges, and deliver them either to the common huntsman appointed for the precinct where they are seized upon, or to the governor of the said precinct.

Dated at Kilkenny, April 27 1652.'

The following year a further notice was issued detailing substantial rewards for whoever would kill wolves.

DECLARATION TOUCHING WOLFES

'For the better destroying of wolfes which of late years have much increased in most parts of this nation, it is ordered that the Commanders-in-chiefe and Commissioners of the Revenue in the several precincts doe consider of, use, and execute all good wayes and meanes how the wolfes in the counties and places within the respective precincts may be taken and destroyed; and to employ such person or persons, and to appoint such daies and tymes for hunting the wolfe, as they shall adjudge necessary. And it is further ordered that all such person or persons as shall take, kill, or destroy any wolfes, and shall bring forth the head of the wolfe before the said Commanders of the Revenue, shall receive the sums following, viz., for every bitch wolfe, six pounds; for every dog wolfe, five pounds; for every cubb which preyeth for himself, forty shillings; for every suckling cubb, ten shillings. And no wolfe after the last

September until the 10th January be accounted a young wolfe, and the Commisioners of the Revenue shall cause the same to be equallie assessed within their precincts.

Dublin, June 29, 1653.'

(Six pounds in 1653 was worth the equivalent of £1,113 today, (2023), so these are considerable incentives.)

One Captain Piers rose to the challenge that same year by obtaining a lease for five years, which cost him £543, of all the forfeited lands in the barony of Dunboyne, Co. Meath, on his proposals for killing wolves and foxes. He proposed to keep:

'...three wolfdogs, two mastiffs, a pack of hounds of sixteen couple, three whereof to hunt the wolf only, a knowing huntsman, and two men and a boy – an orderly hunt to take place thrice a month at least.'

It was in this exceedingly difficult climate that Dorothy Osbourne wrote to Henry Cromwell (Oliver's son), one of her 'admirers', in order to get an Irish greyhound. Henry assured her that he would do so. She received a bitch, but still sought a dog so in 1653 she wrote to her future husband, Sir William Temple:

'You shall do one favour for me. When your father goes into Ireland, lay your commands upon some of his servants to get you an Irish greyhound. I have one that was the General's, (Oliver Cromwell), but tis a bitch, and those are always much less than the dogs. I got it in the time of my favour there, and it was all they had. Henry Cromwell undertook to write to his brother, Fleetwood, for another for me; but I have lost my hopes there. Whomsoever it is that you employ he will need no other instruction, but to get the biggest he can meet with; tis all the beauty of those dogs, or of any kind, I think. A mastiff is handsomer to me than the most exact little dog that ever lady played withal. You will not offer to take it ill that I employ you in such a commission.'

William's father was Sir John Temple, member of the Irish parliament and 'Master of the Rolls' at one time.

Dorothy wrote to William Temple again in 1653:

'As little room as I have left too, I must tell you what a present I had made me today, two of the finest young Irish greyhounds that ere I saw. A gentleman that serves the General sent them to me. They are newly come over, and sent for by Henry Cromwell, he tells me, but not how he got them for me. However, I am glad I have them.'

Alas poor Henry, she married Sir William anyway, ungrateful wench!

Sir William Temple himself gives an interesting insight into the traditions of Ireland's noble families:

'The great men of the Irish septs, among the many officers of their family, which continued always in the same race, had not only a physician, a huntsman, a smith, and such like, but a poet and a tale-teller. The poet recorded and sung the actions of their ancestors and entertained the company at feasts; the tale-teller amused them with tales when they were melancholy and could not sleep. A very gallant gentleman of the North of Ireland has told me, of his own experience, that in the wolf-huntings there, when he used to be in the mountains three or four days together, and lay very ill a-nights, so as he could not well sleep, they would bring him one of these tale-tellers, that, when he lay down, would begin a story of a king, or a giant, a dwarf and a damsel, and such rambling stuff, and continue it all night long in such an even tone, that you heard it going on whenever you awaked; and he believed nothing any physicians give could have so good and so innocent an effect to make men sleep, in any pain or distempers of body or mind.'

Christopher Wase speaks of the Irish greyhound in his translation of Grattius', *Cynegeticon*, in 1654.

'Although we have no wolves in England, yet it is certain that heretofore we had routs of them, as they have at this present in Ireland; in that countrey is bred a race of greyhounds, which is fleet, strong and bears a naturall enmity to the wolfe. Here I would take the boldnesse to examine that 77 Epistle of the second book of Symmachus, where he speaks of Canes Scotici. It is well enough known, that in the age of Claudian, which was near to his, the Irish man had the name of Scotus.

...totum cum Scotus Jernen Moverit.

Now in the greyhounds of that nation, there is incredible force and boldnesse, so that they are much sought for in foreign parts; and the King of Poland (John II r.1648-1668), makes use of them in his hunting of great beasts by force: wherefore it may well be intended of the great fiercenesse which these dogs have in assaulting, that when the Romans saw them play, they thought them so wonderfull violent, as that they must needs have been ferreis caveis advecti.' (transported in iron cages).

Sir James Ware in his, *Antiquities of Ireland*, 1654, writes:

'Those hunting dogs, which are commonly called wolfdogs,

Frontispiece to Sir James Ware's, Antiquities of Ireland. 1654.

from their chasing wolves, must not be passed over by us, they are endowed with extraordinary strength, size and beauty. I shall but just hint at the eagerness of the Irish in the chase, as in hunting wolves and stags.'

In 1656, the first Marquis of Antrim, Randal MacDonnell, wrote to Colonel Robert Steuard:

'Dear Cousin,

I am pressed for a thing for which I would never call to you could I be supplied elsewhere. I must in an extraordinary way beg the favour from you to change your great dog with me for another whom I assure you will be more serviceable to you than your own, and you shall have the advantage more by it, that I shall attribute to you to be the means to contribute to my good fortunes which may be purchased by my presenting this dog. If you refuse me this request, I shall despair of others to supply me. I hope you will not deny Rose, though you should deny me.' (Rose was his second wife and the daughter of Sir Henry O'Neill of Clandeboye).

I think it safe to assume that the dog in question was an Irish wolfdog, as no other large breed at the time would have been so difficult to procure.

The hunting of wolves is mentioned in a letter dated 11th July 1657 from Sir George Rawdon to Viscount Conway:

'...on Monday to find the first passage to Chester; also the dogs which it is a pity to send out of the country, especially one of them. They have been about, 'The Collen' and above Mr. Doynes this six weeks, and had some courses at wolves which exceedingly infest this country.'

The Collen referred to is known today as the Big Collin, a hill in a high moorland area of south Antrim with an area known as Wolf Bog nearby. It seems also that the two men were engaged in the trade of wolfdogs as Rawdon seems reluctant to see them go, being especially fond of one of them.

In 1660, Mrs Katherine Philips, known by her nom de plume, 'Orinda', a friend of the now Dorothy Temple, wrote a poem about an Irish greyhound, probably one of Dorothy's.

The Irish Greyhound

Behold this creature's form and state!
Him Nature surely did create,
That to the world might be exprest
What mien there can be in a beast;
More nobleness of form and mind
Than in the lion we can find:
Yea, this heroic beast doth seem
In majesty to rival him.
Yet he vouchsafes to man to show
His service, and submission too
And here we a distinction have;
That brute is fierce – the dog is brave.
He hath himself so well subdued,
That hunger cannot make him rude;
And all his manners do confess
That courage dwells with gentleness,
War with the wolf he loves to wage,
And never quits if he engage;
But praise him much, and you may chance
To put him out of countenance.
And having done a deed so brave,
He looks not sullen, yet looks grave.
No fondling play-fellow is he;

His master's guard he wills to be:
Willing for him his blood be spent,
His look is never insolent.
Few men to do such noble deeds have learn'd,
Nor having done, could look so unconcern'd.

The 3rd Earl of Winchelsea, Sir Heneage Finch, Ambassador to Constantinople 1660-1669, made a gift of two Irish greyhounds in 1662 to the Sultan, Mehmed IV who reigned from 1648 to 1687. These dogs were quite probably those supplied by the Grand Duke of Tuscany, Cosimo III de Medici, (son and successor to the afore-mentioned Ferdinand), who on behalf of the Levant Company, writing from London to the Earl had said:

'Being some time past minded by your Secretary, and knowing also that such things may be of use there, and no unacceptable present; we send by these ships, two large and comely Irish greyhounds, to be disposed of as your Excellency may see occasion.'

An Irish Greyhound. 1665. From The Book of the Greyhound by Edward Ash.

That wolf hunting was never really a popular pursuit among the wealthy can be illustrated by the fact that a hunting addict like Lord Cork only once mentions a wolf hunt in his diary in 1662. By far the favoured animals were the stag, (male red deer) and the buck, (male fallow deer).

From the *Rawdon Papers*, a set of correspondence from the 17th century, we have an interesting letter from the 3rd Viscount Conway to Sir George Rawdon, his estate manager, at Lisburn, giving an account of a dogfight held before Charles II, between a mastiff and a wolfdog. These are the same two men seen to have previously been engaged in the trade in wolfdogs.

London, 29 October, 1667.
'...We had yesterday an unfortunate passage: Addy Loftus brought an Irish dog to fight with a mastiff before the King; the Irish dog had all the advantage imaginable, and dragged him five or six times about the ring, so that everybody gave the mastiff for dead; all men were concerned as if it had been their General, and yet at last the Irish dog run away; I lost my money; and afterwards the King called me to him, and said he would lay £500 that neither I nor all the men in Ireland could bring an Irish wolfdog that would not run away. I pray speak with my Lord Dungannon, (Marcus Trevor, 1st Viscount Dungannon), about it, for tho' I will not upon any man's confidence venture so much money, yet I will be willing to go my share, and I am sure the King will lay it. I pray speak with my Lord Lieutenant, (James Butler, 1st Duke of Ormonde), and know what dogs he hath, and enquire amongst all your friends, for I would fain recover the credit of our country. I hope I shall hear from you how all affairs go at Dublin, and from hence I shall neglect no opportunity to inform you of all matters, and to assure you of my being

Your's, &c.
Conway

John Dryden, (1631-1700), was the first Poet Laureate, and was probably thinking of Irish greyhounds when he wrote:
'Ten brace, or more, of greyhounds, snowy fair,
And tall as stags ran loose about his chair,
A match for pards in flight, in grappling, for the bear.'

The Diary of John Evelyn provides an interesting account, dated the 16th of June 1669:

'I went with some friends to the Bear Garden, where was cockfighting, dogfighting, bear and bull-baiting, it being a famous day for all these butcherly sports, or rather barbarous cruelties. The bulls, (bulldogs) did exceeding well, but the Irish wolf-dog exceeded, which was a tall greyhound, a stately creature indeed, who beat a cruel mastiff.'

This gives a good indication as to how formidable these dogs were, as the mastiff together with the bulldog were the most formidable canines on the planet. What is surprising is that so valuable a beast would be displayed in the combats of the Bear Garden.

In 1671, Nicholas Jones of Dublin, in a letter to Captain George Legge of London wrote:

'I have endeavoured by all industry and friendship I could, to get you a brace of wolf-dogs, which as yet I cannot possibly procure.'

The Gentleman's Recreation, by Nicholas Cox of 1675 gives a passing mention of the Irish greyhound in his description of the common greyhound.

Irish wolfdog of 1671. From The Book of the Greyhound by Edward Ash.

'Some dogs are very great, as the Wolf-Dog, which is shaped like a Greyhound, but by much taller, longer and thicker;… The best Greyhound hath a long body, strong and reasonably great, not so big as the Wolf-Dog in Ireland.'

A further passage in reference to the wolf-dog is merely a word for word copy of that given by Sir James Ware in 1654.

A little further on in his chapter on foreign methods of hunting, Cox copies Christopher Wase's work of 1654.

'Although we have no Wolves in England at this present, yet it is certain, that heretofore we had routs of them, as they have to this very day in Ireland; and in that country are bred a race of Greyhounds, (which are commonly called Wolf-Dogs), which are strong, fleet, and bear a natural enmity to the Wolf. Now in these the Greyhounds of that nation, there is an incredible force and boldness, so that they are in great estimation, and much sought after in foreign parts, so that the King of Poland makes use of them in his hunting of great beasts by force. Wherefore it may well be intended of the great fierceness which these dogs have in assaulting, that when the Romans saw them play, they thought them so wonderful violent, as that they must needs have been, 'Ferreis caveis advecti', brought up in iron dens.'

James Butler, Duke of Ormond and Lord Lieutenant of Ireland from 1661 to 1669, wrote to his half-brother, Captain George Mathews, in 1678, requesting two dogs and a bitch for his son, Thomas Butler, the Earl of Ossory, to present to the King of Spain, (Charles II, r.1665-1700), and the same for the King of Sweden, (Charles XI, r.1660-1697). It seems it was necessary for the Duke's Secretary, William Ellis, to remind his half-brother about the arrangement in a letter dated 11th March 1678:

'I have received commands from the Earl of Ossory to put you in mind of two wolfdogs and a bitch which his Lordship wrote to you about for the King of Spain; he desires they may be provided and sent with all convenient speed, and that two dogs and a bitch be also gotten for the King of Sweden.'

Thomas Blount, writing in 1680 said:

'The wolves in Ireland of late years are, in a manner, all destroyed, by the diligence of the inhabitants, and the assistance of Irish greyhounds, a wolfdog.'

Also in 1680, Sir Neil O'Neill, 2nd Baronet of Shane's Castle and Killyleagh had his portrait painted together with an Irish greyhound, by the artist John Michael Wright.

To return to Ireland, the following is a tale of Lough Measg,

(Mask), taken from, *A Chorographical Description of West or H-Iar Connaught*, authored by Roderic O' Flaherty in 1684.

'Here is one rarity more, which we may terme the Irish crocodil, whereof one as yet living, about ten years ago, had sad experience. The man was passing the shore just by the waterside, and spyed far off the head of a beast swimming, which he took to have been an otter, and tooke no more notice of it; but the beast it seems there lifted up his head, to discern whereabouts the man was; then diving, swom under water till he struck ground; whereupon he runned out of the water suddenly, and tooke the man by the elbow, whereby the man stooped down, and the beast fastened his teeth in his pate, and dragged him into the water; where the man tooke hold on a stone by chance in his way, and calling to mind he had a knife in his pocket, tooke it out and gave a thrust of it to the beast, which

William O' Brien, 3rd Earl of Inchiquin. 1685. Sir Godfrey Kneller.

thereupon got away from him into the lake. The water about him was all bloody, whether from the beast's bloud or his own, or from both, he knows not. It was of the pitch of an ordinary grey-hound, of a black slimy skin, without hair, as he immagined. Old men acquainted with the lake do tell there is such a beast in it, and that a stout fellow with a wolf dog along with him met the like there once; which after a long struling went away in spite of the man and dog, and was a long time after found rotten in a rocky cave of the lake, as the water decreased. The like, they say, is seen in other lakes of Ireland; they call it Dovarchu, i.e., a water dog, or Anchu, which is the same.'

In his book, *A Voyage to Surat in the Year 1689*, the Reverend John Ovington wrote:

'A couple of Irish wolfdogs were so prized in Persia that they were taken as a welcome and admired present to the Emperor himself. Two more of which, which were given to me, when we put into Kinsale, by the Earl of Inchiquin, (William O' Brien), I disposed of to the East India Company, who despatched them in their ships immediately to the Indies to be bestowed on some of the Eastern Courts.'

The emperor referred to was Shah Suleiman I who ruled Persia from 1666 to 1694.

During the Williamite wars in Ireland a key battle was fought at Aughrim, 12th July 1691, between the Williamite and Jacobite forces. The Jacobites were defeated and it is recorded that a fallen Irish soldier possessed an Irish greyhound, who locating his body on the battlefield, stood guard over it preventing any one from coming near. It was said to have kept up this vigil for seven months, foraging where it could and hunting for itself, after this time scavengers, maggots and the elements had reduced its master to bone, but still the noble dog remained true. The end came when a soldier stationed nearby went for a walk one evening across the battlefield as dusk fell, he chanced upon the only remains left and their sentinel rose to attack, the soldier panicked and fired, ending the faithful hound's long vigil. George Story, a Williamite Chaplain who was at the battle gives us the following account:

'There is a true and remarkable story of a greyhound, belonging to an Irish Officer, the gentleman was killed and stripped in the battle, whose body the dog remained by night and day and tho' he fed on other corpses with the rest of the dogs yet he would not allow them nor anything else to touch his master.

When all the corpses were consumed the other dogs departed, but his dog used to go in the night to adjacent villages for food, and presently return again to the place where his master's bones were only then left, till January following, when one of the Col. Foulkes soldiers being quartered nigh hand and going that way by chance, the dog fearing he came to disturb his master's bones flew upon the soldier who being surprised at the suddenness of the thing unslung his piece then upon his back and killed the poor dog.'

Quite rightly, the noble dog has been immortalised in verse.

The Dog of Aughrim

The day is ours my gallant men
Cried brave but vain St. Ruth
We've won a deathless victory

For liberty and truth
We'll rest the land from
William's grasp
Tho' we're but one to three
We'll make his crew remember long
The Pass of Urrachree.
That though with myriad cannon
They poured their fierce attack
Still with valour and the naked sword
Thrice have we flung them back
They're beaten boys, they're beaten
Still unsheathe your swords again
And on them like an avalanche
And sweep them from the plain
Like thunderbolt upon the foes
The Irish column sped
Athlone's deep stain to wash away
St. Ruth is at their head
And onward rolls that
Wave of death
But God, what means that cry?
St. Ruth the brave sits on his charger
Headless neath the sky
Oh where's the gallant Sarsfield now
Is victory defeat
Oh God in mercy strike us dead!
Twere better than retreat
Oh where is Limerick's hero bold
The chiefless soldiers cry
And scorning flight they wait the dawn
To give them light to die
When Saxon's sons the scene of death
And robbery had fled

An Irish wolfhound sought his lord
Mid heaps of pilfered dead
And strove with more than human love
To rob death of its prize
Then moaned a dirge above his head
And kissed his lips and eyes
When Autumn pencilled Summer's blooms
In tints of Gold and Red
And Winter over hill and dale
A ghostly mantle spread
The weird wind wailed across the moor
And moaned adown the dell
Yet guarded well that noble dog
His master where he fell
Spring timidly was glancing down
Upon the corpse – strewn plain
Where seven months long sentinel
The faithful dog had lain
When carelessly across the moor
An English soldier trod
And paused beneath the only bones
Remaining on the sod
Up sprang the faithful wolf dog
He knew a foe was near
And feared that foe would desecrate
The bones he loved so dear
Fierce and defiant there he stood
The soldier seized with dread
Took aim and fired, the noble dog
Fell on his master dead.

I found a second poem based on the story in an 1883 edition
of the *Munster Express*:

The Dog of Aughrim

Stark, cold, and still, on Kilcommedan hill,
Lie the fallen of Aughrim's field,
Who with fearless front faced the battle's brunt,
With fiery valour steel'd,
In the battle hewn, in thousands strewn,
Lie the brave and the warrior dead,
And the carrion beast and bird, they feast
On that charnel banquet spread.

And now and then o'er their hideous din,
Loud waileth the mournful tones,
(For dead lies his liege on Kilcommedan's ridge),
Where the Dog of Aughrim moans,
On fields of blood, by his master he stood,
Till he fell in the fatal strife,
More staunch and true than when he but knew,
The quiet of domestic life.

The wolfdog fed on the flesh of the dead
That thickly around him lay,
But away he scared, the ghouls, that dared,
But to touch his master's clay.
The skeletons' white glare, a ghastly sight
By the glutinous ghouls stripped bare,
Save one corpse alone untouched is known,
Rotting and mouldering there.

The hideous uproar is heard no more
On the field of the valiant dead,
For the charnel feast at last has ceased,
And the banqueters are fled;

But day and night, on the dismal height,
Thro' summer's sultry glow,
And the autumn nere 'till the winter dress
Envelopes the land in snow.

One dog stays still on the fatal hill,
Spectral, sad, and weeping;
With mournful care o'er his master there,
His gloomy ward he's keeping:
From want grown weak, when small fare he'll seek,
To sooth fell hunger's pain;
With speed he returns to his task and mourns,
In sorrow's saddest strains.

When the wan moon's light silvers the night,
His dismal wail of woe
It wildly floats with loud thrilling notes,
Then dies in weird cadence low.
Then he'd seek repose in a troubled doze,
O'er wearied with grief and care –
Oft he'd start and scowl, and wrathful growl,
Some dream-wrought foe to scare.

But at last one day, where the wolfdog lay,
Passed a Saxon soldier near;
But his path was barred as the dog rushed to guard
The bones of his master dear;
But the musketoon of the Saxon soon
Struck him down by his master's side,
And with last caressing, the relics pressing,
The brave Dog of Aughrim died.

Glashawley

Another veteran of the Williamite wars was, Patrick Sarsfield, the Earl of Lucan, I have read that he supposedly owned Irish greyhounds and was said to have been painted with two of them. I have not been able to track down the picture but an old description of it states:

'In an old print of Patrick Sarsfield, Earl of Lucan, there are two wolf-dogs, which are represented as smooth, prick-eared, and with somewhat bushy tails.'

Irish wolfdogs had apparently been popular heraldic symbols, supporting the arms of the old Irish kings either collared or with the motto:

'Gentle when stroked – fierce when provoked'

A Belfast schoolmaster in 1823, by the name of J. Compton produced, *A Compendius System of Chronology*, which recorded for the year 1692:

'The last wolf seen in Ireland is killed with Irish wolf-dogs on the hill of Aughnabrack, near Belfast, by Clotworthy Upton, of Castle-Upton, Templepatrick.'

(Aughnabrack, translates as, 'the hill of the wolf,' more commonly known today as Wolf Hill).

In 1697, John Ray, the eminent naturalist gave us this description of the Irish greyhound:

'The greatest dog I have yet seen, surpassing in size even the mollossus, (mastiff), as regards shape of body and general character, is the Irish greyhound, similar in all respects to the common greyhound; their use is to catch wolves.'

John Dunton, the English bookseller and author, who wrote, *Teague Land: A Merry Ramble to the Wild Irish*, visited the summer home of Sir Murrough Na Mart O' Flaherty, (Murrough of the Market), leader of the O' Flaherty clan, and grandson of the famous Grace O'Malley, in 1698 and made mention of the Irish greyhounds owned by his host:

'...a paire of which kind has been often a present for a king, as they are said to be a dog that is peculiar to Ireland, for I am told they breed much better here than anywhere else in the Kingdom. They were as quiet among us as lambs without any noys or disturbance. I enquir'd the use of them and was told that besides the ornament that they were, they kill'd as many deer as pay'd eerie well for their keeping.'

And that,

'...after dinner myn host ordered his dogs to be gotten ready to hunt the stag. He had his horse saddled and one for me too... Eighteen long greyhounds and above thirty footemen made up the company.'

By 1698 wolves had declined to such an extant that Alderman J. Howel of Cork wrote:

'Wolves indeed we have and foxes, but these are now rather game and diversion than noxious or hateful.'

William King, archbishop of Dublin received some Irish geyhounds sometime after his appointment in 1703.

In 1707, Lady Frances Bellew, (neé Wentworth and a descendant of Thomas Wentworth), wrote to her brother Baron Raby warning him about the feeding costs of keeping Irish wolfdogs.

Bas-relief from Castle of Ardnaglass. Circa 1700. Depicting a wolfdog killing a wolf.

A Mr. Windle, writing of southern counties, stated that the last wolf seen in Ireland was killed in the neighbourhood of Annascuit, (Annascaul), near Dingle, in 1710, and that the place thereafter became known as the, 'Wolf's Step'. An Irish term for the wolfdog was said to be 'Sagh cliun'. The 'Wolf's Step' is a flat rock that fords a stream in the area.

It has to be said that several areas in Ireland claim to be where the last wolf was killed and it is too late to fact-check these stories, but what is a fact is that the last claim for a wolf-bounty was in 1710.

It is said that around this time, Augustus II, King of Poland, (r.1709-1733), bought up as many wolfdogs as he could find here. Peter the Great, Czar of Russia, (r.1696-1725), is also said to have acquired Irish wolfdogs at this time.

Edmund Hogan, in his book, *The History of the Irish Wolfdog*, published in 1897, stated:

'Mr. R.D. O'Brien says that there is at Dromoland a picture of Inchiquin, Governor of Kinsale, by Sir Godfrey Kneller. He is represented, in 1719, fondling the head of a huge dog. This is probably a wolfdog, as we see the Earl had that Irish breed.'

The personage referred to here was William O' Brien, the 3rd Earl of Inchiquin, but the painting must have been done quite a few years prior to 1719 as that was the year the Earl died at the age of fifty-seven and he is a young man in the portrait.

Mention is made in Edward Jesse's, *Anecdotes of Dogs*, of a wolf hunt taking place in the counties of Leitrim and Sligo, supposedly early in the 18th century. The source of the story was a Mr. Charles T. Webber, who in February 1841, presented a stone on which was a bas-relief of a dog killing a wolf, to the Royal Irish Academy. The stone said to have come from the castle of Ardnaglass, in the barony of Tireragh, County Sligo and to commemorate the destruction of said wolf.

'The current tradition in the place from whence it came was, that some years after it was supposed that the race of wolves was extinct, the flocks in the county of Leitrim were attacked by a wild animal, which turned out to be a wolf; that there upon the chiefs of Leitrim applied to O'Dowd, the chieftain of Tireragh, (who possessed a celebrated dog of the breed of the ancient Irish wolf-dog), to come and hunt the wolf. This application having been complied with by O'Dowd, there ensued a chase, which forms the subject of an ancient Irish legend, detailing the various districts through which it was pursued, until at length the wolf was overtaken and killed in a small wood of pine trees, at the foot of one of the mountains of Tireragh. The quarter of land on which the wolf was killed is to this day called Carrow na Madhoo, which means, 'the dog's quarter'. In commemoration of the event, O'Dowd had a representation of it carved on stone, and placed in the wall of his baronial residence. It is difficult to form an opinion of the shape of a dog from so rude a representation, except that it appears to have had a wide forehead and pricked ears.'

Jesse goes on to say:

'A gentleman, who in his youth saw one of these dogs, informs me that it was smooth, strong, and partaking somewhat of the character and appearance of a powerful Danish dog.'

There are many accounts throughout Ireland of when and where the last wolf was killed, all generally depending on which part of the country you are in. However, there is an account in the biography of a family from county Tyrone, published in Belfast in 1829, which, tells us of the last wolves to be killed in that county.

'In the mountainous parts of the County Tyrone the inhabitants suffered much from the wolves, and gave from the public fund as much for the head of one of these animals as they would now give for the capture of a notorious robber on the highway. There lived in those days an adventurer, who, alone and unassisted, made it his occupation to destroy these ravagers. The time for attacking them was in the night, and midnight was the best time for doing so, as that was their wonted time for leaving their lair in search of food, when the country was at rest and all was still; then issuing forth, they fell on their defenceless prey, and the carnage commenced. There was a species of dog for the purpose of hunting them, called the wolf-dog; the animal resembled a rough, stout, half-bred greyhound, but was much stronger. In the County Tyrone there was then a large space of ground enclosed by a high stone wall, having a gap at each of the two opposite extremities, and in this were secured the flocks of the surrounding farmers. Still, secure though this fold was deemed, it was entered by the wolves, and its inmates slaughtered. The neighbouring proprietors having heard of the noted wolf-hunter above mentioned, by name Rory Carragh, sent for him, and offered the usual reward, with some addition, if he would undertake to destroy the two remaining wolves that had committed such devastation. Carragh undertaking the task, took with him two wolf-dogs, and a little boy only twelve years old, the only person who would accompany him, and repaired at the approach of midnight to the fold in question. "Now", said Carragh to the boy, "as the two wolves usually enter the opposite extremities of the sheep-fold at the same time, I must leave you and one of the dogs to guard this one while I go to the other. He steals with all the caution of a cat, nor will you hear him, but the dog will, and positively will give him the first fall; if, therefore, you are not active when he is down to rivet his neck to the ground with this spear, he will rise up and kill both you and the dog. So good night."

"I'll do what I can," said the little boy, as he took the spear from the wolf-hunter's hand.

The boy immediately threw open the gate of the fold, and took his seat in the inner part, close to the entrance; his faithful companion crouching at his side, and seeming perfectly aware of the dangerous business he was engaged in. The night was very dark and cold, and the poor little boy being benumbed with the chilly air, was beginning to fall into a kind of sleep, when at that instant the dog with a roar leapt across him, and laid his mortal enemy upon the earth. The boy was roused into double activity by the voice of his companion, and drove the spear through the wolf's neck as he had been directed, at which time Carragh appeared, bearing the head of the other.'

This story does have a ring of truth about it, the fold being a high, round, stone-walled enclosure is a perfect description of a cashel, used by our forebearers for defence in times of trouble and to safeguard livestock. Although many of these were demolished to provide stone for dwellings in later times, there is still an enclosure marked on the Ordnance Survey map just a mile and a half north-east of Cookstown in Tyrone, with a remote location called, 'The Wolf's Hill', six miles north-west of it. Again, the nocturnal nature of the wolves is to be expected in an increasingly populated and hostile countryside and the Sperrin Mountains ranging through Tyrone would have provided ample wilderness for wolves to exist longer than in other more cultivated counties.

In 1733, a Dr R. James, in a treatise on, *Canine Madness,* (probably rabies), referred to:

'...an Irish wolfdog of uncommon size. The dog attacked his owner's child, and would have killed it, but that the dog wore a garland...a garland is a thing well known to sportsmen, and consists of two hoops crossing each other, and which, hanging before a dog's forelegs, prevent his running after sheep, or being otherwise mischievous.'

The Swedish naturalist, Carl Linnaeus, classified dogs in his multi-volume, *Systema Naturae,* of 1735; referring to the Irish greyhound as, Canis Hibernicus.

Linnaeus Classification

Canis familiaris or Faithful Dog
Canis domestic or Shepherd's Dog
Canis Pomeranus or Pomeranian
Canis sibericus or Siberian Dog
Canis islandicus or Iceland Dog
Canis aquaticus major or Great Water Dog (Grand Barbet)
Canis pilosus or Hairy Maltese Dog
Canis leoninus or Lion Dog
Canis variegatus or Little Danish Dog
Canis aquatilis or Barbet
Canis fricator or Pug Dog
Canis molossus or Bulldog
Canis anglicus (bellicosus) or Mastiff
Canis sagax or German Hound
Canis gallicus or Hound
Canis scoticus or Bloodhound
Canis aquaticus minor or Lesser Water Dog
Canis extratius/Canis hyspanicus or Spaniel
Canis hibernicus or Irish Hound
Canis turcicus or Turkish Hound
Canis graius or Scotch Hunting Dog
Canis graius hirsutus or Rough Scotch Hunting Dog
Canis hybridus or Bastard Pug Dog also called Roquet
Canis orientalis or Persian Greyhound
Canis egyptius or Hairless Greyhound
Canis laniarius or Lurcher
Canis Italicus or Italian Greyhound
Canis vertigus or Turnspit
Canis americanus or the Ala
Canis antarcticus or New Holland Dog
Canis fuillius or Boarhound

Canis avicularis or Pointer
Canis cursorius or Greyhound
Canis parvus melitans or Little Maltese Dog

In 1738, the celebrated German natural history artist, Johann Elias Ridinger, began publishing a series of volumes called, *Enturfweiniger Thiere*. Volume 1 contains 18 plates of dogs, plate 7 being the common greyhound, plate 9 the Turkish greyhound, and plate 8 the 'Grosse Irlandisch Windspiel', (large Irish greyhound). There is very little text and the only specific reference to the Irish greyhound is that they:

'...are excellent for overtaking a swift stag.'

Charles Smith, (1715-1762), who wrote, *The Ancient and Present State of the County and City of Waterford*, in 1746, had the following to say:

'The Irish greyhound, though formerly abounding in this country, is likewise become nearly extinct. I have known twenty-five guineas to be paid for a brace of them. This dog is much taller than the mastiff, but made more like a greyhound, and for size, strength, and shape cannot be equalled.'

(It is at least consistent with Ray's description)

Around 1748, in the reign of George II, the Irish historian and author Walter Harris, who translated the complete works of Sir James Ware, stated:

'The English mastiff was in no way comparable to the Irish wolfdog in size and shape. The Irish wolfdog has been thought a valuable present to the greatest monarchs, and is sought after and sent abroad to all quarters of the world. This has been one

Groß Irländisch Windspiel
N. 8.

Large Irish Greyhound. 1738. Johann Elias Ridinger.

cause why this noble creature has grown so scarce among us, as another is the neglect of the species since the extinction of the wolf.'

That the Irish greyhound was becoming increasingly difficult to obtain can be seen in the letter from the 4th Earl Chesterfield, Philip Dormer Stanhope, to a noble French lady, dated 1750:

'I have been trying for these two years to get some of those large dogs of Ireland; but the breed is grown extremely rare there by the extinction of their enemies, the wolves. I had two sent to me six months ago, which I intended to give to the Prince de Conti, but I discovered that in them was a mixture of the Danish breed which had made them clumsy, so I sent them back again. I expect soon some of the true kind, which I shall do myself the honour to send over immediately to his Highness. Meanwhile I beg you to send orders to somebody at Calais to receive them, and let me know who I am to direct them to. I shall always be glad to be of any service to a Prince of his merit.
London, 7th December, 1750.'

The Prince de Conti in question being, Louis Francois de Bourbon, (r.1727-1776).

The future 2nd Earl of Altamont, Peter Browne, was painted with an Irish greyhound around 1750 by the artist Thomas Gibson.

From, *The Gentleman's Magazine*, by Sylvanus Urban of 1834, we have the following information taken from a work by Richard Barton:

'In a dialogue entitled, *'Some Things of Importance to Ireland'*, published in Dublin in 1751, the author states, that an old man, near Lurgan, informed him, that when he was a boy, wolves during winter, used to come within two miles of that town, and destroy cattle. This must have been about the beginning of the last century, (17th century).

According to several accounts, the last wolf observed in

Peter Browne of Kinturk, Co. Mayo, with an Irish wolfhound. 1750.
Thomas Gibson? Last known to be in the collection of the late Knight of
Glynn.

Ireland was killed in the county of Kerry, in 1710; another
tradition says on the Crany river, Carnlough, near Glenarm;
and another account adds, that the last wolf seen in Ulster,
was shot by Arthur Upton, on Aughnabreack, or the Wolf-hill,
near Belfast.'

William Guthrie in his *Geographical Grammar,* of 1770, said:

'Irish wolfdogs, which are much larger than mastiffs, shaped
like a greyhound yet as gentle and governable as spaniels.'

107

Richard Brookes, in his, *A New and Accurate System of Natural History*, of 1772, stated:

'The Irish wolfdog is, as 'Ray', affirms, the highest dog he had ever seen, being much larger than a mastiff dog but more like a greyhound in shape. These are the dogs once made use of in that country for catching wolves, and might more properly be called wolf dogs.'

The naturalist, Oliver Goldsmith, produced his eight-volume work, *Animated Nature*, in 1774 and in the section dealing with dogs gives a very interesting eyewitness account of the Irish greyhound.

'The last variety and the most wonderful of all that I shall mention, is the great Irish wolfdog, that may be considered as the first of the canine species. This animal, which is very rare even in the only country of the world where it is to be found, is rather kept for show than use, there being neither wolves nor any other formidable beasts of prey in Ireland that seem to require so powerful an antagonist. The wolfdog is, therefore, bred up in the houses of the great, or such gentlemen as choose to keep him as a curiosity, being neither good for hunting the hare, the fox, nor the stag, and equally unserviceable as a house dog. Nevertheless, he is extremely beautiful and majestic as to appearance, being the greatest of the dog kind to be seen in the world. The largest of those I have seen, and I have seen above a dozen, was about four feet high, or as tall as a calf of a year old. He was made extremely like a greyhound, but rather more robust, and inclining to the figure of the French matin, or the Great Dane. His eye was mild, his colour white, and his nature seemed heavy and phlegmatic. This I ascribe to his having been bred up to a size beyond his nature; for we see in man, and all other animals, that such as are overgrown are neither so vigorous nor alert as those of more moderate stature. The greatest pains have been taken with these to enlarge the breed, both by food and matching. This end was effectually obtained, for the size was enormous; but, as it seemed to me, at the expense of the animal's fierceness, vigilance and sagacity. However, I was informed otherwise; the gentleman who bred them assuring me that a mastiff would be nothing when opposed to one of them, who generally seized their antagonist by the back; he added, that they would worry the strongest bulldogs in a few minutes to death. But this strength did not appear either in their figure or their inclinations; they seemed rather more timid than the ordinary race of dogs, and their skin was much thinner and consequently less fitted for combat. Whether with these disadvantages they were capable, as I was told, of single coping with bears, others may determine; however, they have but few opportunities in their own country of exerting their strength, as all wild carnivorous animals there are only of the vermin kind. Mr. Buffon seems to be of the opinion that they are the true Molossian dogs of the ancients; he gives no reason for this opinion, and I am apt to think it ill-grounded. Not to trouble the reader with a tedious critical disquisition, which I have all along avoided, it will be sufficient to observe that Nemesianus, in giving direction for the choice of a bitch, advises to have one of Spartan or Molossian breed; and among several other perfections, he says that the ears should be dependant and fluctuate as she runs. This, however, is by no means the case with the Irish wolfdog, whose ears resemble those of the greyhound, and are far from fluctuating with the animal's motions. But of whatever kind these dogs may be, whether known among the ancients, or whether produced by a later mixture, they are now almost quite worn away, and are very rarely to be met with even in Ireland. If carried to other countries they soon degenerate, and even at home, unless great care be taken, they quickly alter. They were once employed in clearing the land of wolves, which infested it in great plenty; but these being destroyed, the dogs are also wearing away, as if nature meant to blot out the species, when they had no longer any services to perform.'

I came across a story in my research of Oliver Goldsmith's mother having a close encounter with a wolf as a young girl. It relates that she had taken a walk on a winter's day to visit a relative and was returning home when at a very lonely spot on her journey a gaunt, lean, hungry wolf made toward her but she was saved by an Irish greyhound who attacked the wolf and left it dying by the roadside. In one version of the story the dog was called 'Bran' and belonged to her family and in another the dog appeared out of nowhere. I have not been able to locate the original source of the story though.

Also in 1774, the naturalist Schreber, included a painting of an Irish greyhound in full colour showing a mainly white dog with tan patches, plate 87, Volume 3 of his, *Die Säugthiere in Abbildungen nach der Natur*. However, it is nothing more than a colourised version of the Ridinger engraving of 1738.

A year after this, 1775, Richard Twiss wrote in his, *A Tour in Ireland*:

'The last wolf was killed in this country in 1710; since which time, none of those animals have been found in Ireland. The Irish wolf-dog, which formerly abounded here, is now become nearly extinct. I saw two of them in Dublin; they were much taller than a mastiff, or than any dog I had seen, and appeared to be of great strength. Their

Canis familiaris. 1774. Johann Christian Dan Schreber. A colourised copy of the Ridinger engraving.

shape was somewhat like that of a greyhound; they were the property of a nobleman, and were valued at twenty guineas each.' (£2,779 in today's money – 2023).

Again, in 1775 the French naturalist, Buffon, also attempted the classification of dogs, drawing up the following table:

Buffon Classification

Bulldog
Iceland Hound
Wolf Dog
Terrier

Large Spaniel
Small Spaniel
Lapland Dog
Shepherd Dog
Hound
Small Water Dog
Siberian Hound
Harrier
Water Dog
Mastiff
Large Danish Dog
Irish Greyhound
English Greyhound
Large Greyhound
Great Hound Mongrel

Going on to say:

'The Irish greyhounds are of very ancient race and still exist, though in small numbers in their original climate… These dogs are much larger than the mastiff; they are so rare in France that I never saw but one of them, and he appeared as he sat to be about five feet high, and in form resembled the large Danish dog; but exceeded him very much in his size. He was quite white, and his manner was perfectly gentle and peaceable…The Irish greyhound, the large Dane, and the common greyhound, have, besides the resemblance of form and long snout, the same dispositions; they love to course and to follow horses; they have but indifferent noses, and hunt rather from their sight than their scent.'

I have come across mention in my research of an Irish wolfdog kept by Buffon having killed the wolf it was raised with. This, however, is completely inaccurate. Buffon never owned an example of the breed, he states himself that he never saw but one. The dog in his experiment was a French matin, a powerful type of hunting dog, which did indeed end up killing the wolf it had lived with.

Also in 1775, William Bowles, who had been born in a village near Cork, published, whilst living in Spain, *An Introduction to the Natural History of Spain*. In 1752, he had been employed by the Spanish Government to establish and direct a Museum of Natural History. In his chapter on Biscay he wrote:

'In the woods may be met with by chance a wild boar. The ordinary wolves, (lobos comunes) are rare…Should one be seen he is at once hunted and killed, for which work are excellent the greyhounds, (perros lebreles), which they have brought hither from Ireland.'

So it would seem that Irish greyhounds had been exported to Spain for the task of hunting wolves.

Thomas Pennant in his, *British Zoology*, of 1777 stated:

'The Irish gre-hound, a dog now extremely scarce in that kingdom, the late king of Poland having procured from thence as many as possible. I have seen two or three in the whole island: they were of the kind called by M. de Buffon, Le grand Danois, and probably imported there by the Danes who long possessed that kingdom. Their use seems originally to have been for the chace of wolves with which Ireland swarmed until the latter half of the seventeenth century. As soon as those animals were extirpated, the numbers of the dogs decreased; from that period, they were kept only for state.'

Pennant attributed the lack of wolfdogs in Ireland to the late King of Poland buying up as many as he could. I have read elsewhere that it was a King John of Poland who was the culprit; however, the last Polish king to die before Pennant's work was published in 1777 was Augustus III, who reigned from 1734 until his death in 1763. By this time certainly the Irish greyhound had become extremely rare.

The artist, Gabriel Beranger, a Dutch Hugenot who moved to Dublin in 1750, made antiquarian tours through Ireland. During one such tour through the west of Ireland in 1779 he described the Irish greyhound:

'On the 17th July, Lord Altamont after dinner showed us, (Beranger and Bigari), his wolfdogs, three in number; they are amazing large, white, with black spots, but of the make and shape of the greyhound, only the head and neck somewhat larger in proportion.'

This would have been at Westport House, the family home, and the Lord Altamont in question was the 2nd Earl, Peter Browne, who incidentally had a portrait of himself with an Irish greyhound painted by Thomas Gibson.

In 1786, the last wolf in Ireland was said to have been killed at Myshall in County Carlow, by a Mr. Watson. The wolf had been hunted down from Mount Leinster where it had been killing sheep, by a hound pack and met its end on the bank of a stream. I have to say I have extreme doubts about this story. If it did happen at all, I cannot believe the wolf in question was a truly wild Irish wolf. It seems much more likely to me that the animal, if it was a wolf and not just a feral dog, was probably acquired from a circus or menagerie and released for the express purpose of being hunted.

I researched the archives of Irish newspapers going back to

1738 and did not find a single account of a wolf being killed in Ireland. These papers reported wolf attacks and hunts being carried out in America, France, Germany, Switzerland, Hungary and Russia and yet not one of them mentioned a wolf hunt taking place in their own country. Why? Such an event would have been headline news, especially the demise of the very last Irish wolf. The answer can only be because no such event occurred. The most reliable date for the demise of the Irish wolf in my opinion has to be prior to 1734 and as I have already mentioned, the last wolf bounty was claimed in 1710 and this kill would necessarily have been verified before the bounty would be paid. Therefore 1710 is the date I would suggest that the Irish wolf became extinct.

Another reference to the Irish greyhound comes from the *Dublin University Magazine Vol. XVI*, of 1840, referring to events, which occurred in the life of one George Robert Fitzgerald. A wealthy landowner of Turlough, Co. Mayo. This gentleman certainly had a wild side and although a member of the Protestant ascendancy, would find himself on the gallows as a result of orchestrating two murders over a private quarrel. Fitzgerald had a strong dislike for the Brownes of Westport House, (the Earls of Altamont), the most influential family in Mayo, firing shots at members more than once and generally baiting them whenever he got the chance as the following incident, which occurred in the 1780s' in the time of the 3rd Earl of Altamont, records.

'George Robert rode up to Westport House, asked to see the wolf-dog, an animal so large and fierce, that he was at the same time the admiration and terror of the neighbourhood. Now just then his Lordship's brother, a huge man as the Browne family are disposed to be, enjoyed the high office of prime sergeant in the law courts, and was considered as the great lawyer of the family – for in those days it was particularly expedient for one member of a family to be at the bar, in order to bark and bite when occasion required. Now Mr. Browne being the BIG BOW-WOW of the Brownes, it was not a bad hit for the Westportians to name the huge watch-dog of the house the prime sergeant. Well, the minute George Robert was shewn the dog, he instantly shot him, and desired the servants to tell their master, that until the noble peer became charitable to the poor, who now came to his door only to be barked at and bit by the overfed monster, and which devoured the broken meat which should have been bestowed on them; he could not allow any such brute to be kept. He however left a note to say, that as he always felt for the ladies, he would allow Lady Anne, Lady Elizabeth, and Lady Charlotte Browne, to have each one lap-dog. Proud of his exploit, he rode into the adjoining town of Westport, and proclaimed in the marketplace that he had shot the prime sergeant. This announcement raised the whole populace. Everyone had heard of George Robert's exploit as a manslayer in duels; and now in their alarm and horror it was debated whether the homicide should not instantly be seized. Yes, by all means; but who was to bell the cat – who would come forward to lay hand on this ready pistoller and swordsman. But while thus hesitating he quieted all by saying –

'Gentlemen, don't be alarmed for your big counsellor. I have shot a much worthier animal, the big watch-dog.'

George Robert Fitzgerald was hanged in Castlebar in 1786.

Richard Gough in his 1789 edition of William Camden's *Britannia*, states:

'Under the article of greyhounds Mr. Camden seems to place the wolf-dogs, which are remarkably large and peculiar to this kingdom, (Ireland). The race is now almost extinct: there are not perhaps, ten in the country. Greyhounds are mentioned in the Brehon laws…The Earl of Altamont, at his seat at Westport, in the county of Mayo, possesses a few of the true Irish wolf-dog, a species of animal peculiar to this kingdom, and formerly made use of for destroying that fierce animal the wolf, and even considered as worthy the acceptance of kings. But they are now nearly extinct. They are a large, noble, handsome animal, remarkably quiet, patient in anger till really provoked; but then truly formidable, their hair standing erect, and they never quit their hold but with certain destruction. They hunt both by scent and sight, and are generally about three feet high, sometimes larger; white, or white with a few black or brown spots.'

The Irish greyhound appears in Thomas Bewick's, *A General History of Quadrupeds*, in 1790. Bewick, justly famous for his fine woodcarvings, includes one depicting a male of the breed, with the following information:

'The Irish greyhound is the largest of the dog kind, and its appearance the most beautiful. It is only to be found in Ireland, and is now extremely rare. These dogs are about three feet high, generally of a white or cinnamon colour, somewhat like a greyhound, but more robust. Their aspect is mild, their disposition peaceable, their strength so great that in combat the mastiff or bulldog is far from being equal to them. They mostly seize their antagonist by the back, and shake them to death, which their great strength enables them to do.'

Irish Greyhound. 1790. From A General History of Quadrupeds, by Thomas Bewick.

The antiquary, Reverend Samuel Pegge, writing in, *Archaeologia Volume X*, page 160, of 1792, states that he had seen some.

> 'And indeed I have formerly seen a strong, and yet swift, kind of greyhound, which they termed a wolf-dog. There was one at Lambeth Palace, and another at Wentworth House; and if the breed be not now quite worn out, perhaps it may be found in Ireland or Scotland.'

(Lambeth Palace, the Archbishop of Canterbury's official London residence and Wentworth House, home to the 4th Earl Fitzwilliam. Although interestingly it had been the home of Thomas Wentworth, 1st Earl of Strafford who had been Lord Deputy of Ireland in 1632, and as previously mentioned, had been painted twice with an Irish greyhound by Van Dyck in 1633 and 1639).

One of Lord Altamont's dogs is described in detail by Aylmer Bourke Lambert in a paper read before the Linnaean Society 1st April 1794.

'This drawing was given me by Lord Altamont, done exactly the natural size of one in his lordship's possession at Westport, in the County of Mayo, Ireland, during my stay there, in 1790. I had frequent opportunities of observing these dogs, Lord Altamont having eight of them, the only ones now in the kingdom. There is a man kept on purpose to take care of them, as they are with difficulty bred up and kept healthy. I took the measurements of one of the largest, which are as follows: From the tip of the nose to the end of the tail, 61 in.; tail, 17 ½ in. long; from the tip of the nose to the back part of the skull, 10 in.; from the back part of the skull to the beginning of the tail, 33 in.; from the toe of the foreleg to the top of the shoulders, 28 ½ in.; the length of the leg, 16 in.; from the point of the nose to the first point of the eye, 4 ½ in.; the ear, 6 in. long; round the widest part of the belly, about 3 in. from the legs, 35 in. – 26 in. round the hind part, close to the hind legs. The hair, short and smooth; the colour, brown and white of some, others black and white. They seem good-natured animals, but, from the account I received, are now degenerated in size, having been larger some years ago, and their make more like a greyhound. – A.B.L.'

When we compare this account with Beranger's of 1779, things have changed with Lord Altamont's wolfdogs. In the eleven years since, they increased from three to eight in number and seemed to have lost quite a lot of their greyhound makeup. Of course the increase could easily be explained by breeding but the change in appearance would seem to indicate a cross.

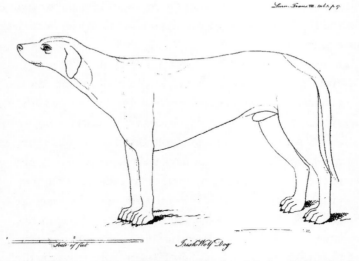

Irish Wolf Dog. 1790. A drawing presented to A.B. Lambert by Lord Altamont.

The following excerpt is taken from, *Transactions of the Linnean Society, Volume III* of 1797.

'Jan. 3, 1797. The following extract of a letter from the Earl of Altamont to A.B. Lambert, Esq. Vice President of the Linnean Society was read to the Society.

There were found in Ireland two kinds of wolfdogs, the greyhound and the mastiff. Till within these two years I was possessed of both kinds, perfectly distinct and easily known from each other. The heads were not so sharp in the latter as in the former, but there seemed a great similarity of temper and disposition, both being harmless and indolent. The painting in your possession is of the mastiff wolfdog. (See tab. 3, of the present volume).

I have at present five wolfdogs remaining, three males and two females; in these the two sorts appear to be mixed. The dam was of the mastiff, the sire if I am not mistaken, was of the greyhound kind. The sire and dam had not dwindled in size from any that I remember here. Those that now remain are too young to judge of. We have an old man here, named Bryan Scahil, now in his 119th year, whose memory seems accurate, and all his faculties complete. He perfectly remembers the hunting of wolves in Ireland, as a common matter of sport, and informs me that the usage was to collect all the dogs of every sort in the neighbourhood, and to borrow wolfdogs from the principal gentlemen, who alone had them, and who usually assisted in the chace. A tenth part of the dogs used were not wolf-dogs, which never were in any number in the hands of the common people. I conceive also that these dogs having no nose, other kinds were necessary to find the game and follow the scent of it. Scahil described wolves with such perfect accuracy, I have no doubt of his being well acquainted with the animal.'

Although Altamont states that there were two kinds of wolfdog in Ireland, I have not come across any evidence to support this view, all other contemporary accounts have been consistent in describing a greyhound type dog. The picture he refers to of the mastiff wolfdog would seem to indicate a cross of some sort, possibly with the mastiff or a large scent hound, such as those which became known as staghounds. When a breed had grown so few in number it would be natural to look for fresh blood to try to enlarge the gene pool and counteract the effects of very close inbreeding, which, without having large numbers to cull through would soon prove detrimental to physical and mental well-being. This cross may well have taken place before the Earl's time and been kept quiet. In those days purity in highly bred horses, game fowl and hounds was something which was religiously adhered to and fresh blood only introduced when absolutely necessary. Owners also were very jealous of their stock and would seldom part with an individual for love or money and so through time isolated pockets would develop, becoming increasingly smaller, dwindling in health and vigour until they became extinct.

Edward Jesse, in his, *Anecdotes of Dogs*, presents us with the following story about the Irish wolfdog, said to have taken place around 1800, albeit it does smack of a tale, rather than a factual account.

'A gentleman of an ancient family, whose name it is unnecessary to mention, from his having been engaged in the troubles which agitated Ireland about fifty or sixty years since, (United Irishmen uprising), went into a coffee-room at Dublin during that period, accompanied by a noble wolf-dog, supposed to be one of the last of the breed. There was only one other gentleman in the coffee-room, who, on seeing the dog, went up to him, and began to notice him. His owner, in considerable alarm, begged him to desist, as the dog was fierce and would never allow a stranger to touch him. The gentleman resumed his seat, when the dog came to him, showed the greatest pleasure at being noticed, and allowed himself to be fondled. His owner could not disguise his astonishment. "You are the only person," he said, "whom that dog would ever allow to touch him without showing resentment. May I beg of you the favour to tell me your name?" – mentioning his own at the same time. The stranger announced it, (he was the last of his race, one of the most ancient and noble in Ireland, and descended from one of its kings). "I do not wonder," said the owner of the dog, "at the homage this animal has paid to you. He recognises in you the descendant of one of our most ancient race of gentlemen to whom this breed of dogs almost exclusively belonged, and the peculiar instinct he possesses has now been shown in a manner which cannot be mistaken by me, who am so well acquainted with the ferocity this dog has hitherto shown to all strangers.'"

Jesse presents us with another recollection of the wolfdog from the pen of Mrs. S. Carter Hall, again dating back to around 1800.

'When I was a child, I had a very close friendship with a genuine old wolf-dog, Bruno by name. He was the property of an old friend of my grandmother's, who claimed descent from the Irish kings. His name was O'Toole. His manners were the most courtly you can imagine; as well they might be, for he had spent much time and fortune at the French court, when Marie Antoinette was in her prime and beauty, (1770-1792). His visits were my jubilees – there was the kind, old dignified gentleman, who told me tales – there was his tall, gaunt dog, grey with age, and yet with me full of play; and there were two rough terriers, whom Bruno kept in admirable order. He managed the little one by simply placing his paw on it when it was too frisky; but Vixen, the large one, like many ladies had a will of her own, and entertained some idea of being mistress. Bruno would bear a good deal from her, giving, however, now and then, a low deep growl; but when provoked too much, he would quietly lift the dog off the ground by the strength of his jaws, (his teeth were gone), stand with her in his mouth at the doors until they were opened, and then deposit her, half strangled as she was, in a nettle-bed some distance from the house. The dog's discrimination was curious. If Vixen was thrown upon him, or if we forced her to insult him, he never punished her; but if she of her own accord teased him more than his patience could bear, the punishment was sure to follow.

O'Toole and his dogs always occupied the same room, the terriers being on the bed with their master. No entreaty, however, ever induced Bruno to sleep on anything softer than stone. He would remove the hearthrug and lay on the marble. His master used to instance the dog's disdain of luxury as a mark of his noble nature.

I should not omit to tell you, as characteristic of my old friend, that O'Toole was proud, and never would submit to being called 'Mr'. Meeting, one day, Lord Arne in Dame Street, Dublin, while the old man was followed by his three wolf-dogs, of which Bruno was the last, the young nobleman, who had also his followers in the shape of, 'Parliament men', said to the descendant of Irish kings, nodding to him familiarly at the same time, "How do you do Mr. O'Toole?" The old man paused, drew himself up, lifted his hat, made his courtly bow, and answered, "O'Toole salutes Arne." I can recall nothing more picturesque than that majestic old gentleman and his dog, both remnants of a bygone age. Bruno was rough, but not long-coated, very grave, observant, enduring everyone, very fond of children, playing with them gently, but only crouching and fawning on his master; "and that," O'Toole would say, "is a proof of my royal blood." I could fill a volume with memoirs of that fine old man. He was more than six feet in height, and his dog always sat with his head on his master's knee.'

Although Mrs. Hall describes Bruno as being rough-coated, there is a sketch of O'Toole meeting Arne in Jesse's book, and the three huge wolfdogs following him are all smooth-coated. Perhaps she was referring to the coat's texture rather than length. Indeed, I have in my research come across a reference of a bloodhound's coat being described as rough, but at the same time smooth, hence it

O'Toole salutes Arne. From, Anecdotes of Dogs, 1846, by Edward Jesse.

was the feel of the coat which was rough. My own greyhound had a soft, velvety, coat, whereas a friend's Rhodesian ridgeback, had a thicker, much coarser coat, both are smooth-coated breeds but there is a big difference in texture.

Quoting Jesse once again, we are given further proof as to how formidable the wolfdog was.

> 'The strength of these dogs must have been very great. A nobleman informed me, that when he was a boy, and staying on a visit with the Knight of Kerry, two Irish wolf-dogs made their escape from the place in which they were confined, and pulled down and killed a horse, which was in an adjoining paddock.'

The Knight in question being most likely, Maurice Fitzgerald, 18th Knight of Kerry who held the title from 1781 to his death in 1849.

Our next mention is in, *The Sportsman's Cabinet*, by William Taplin published in 1803.

'The dog originally distinguished by this appellation, (Irish greyhound), is, in the present age, so rarely to be seen, that it is a matter of doubt whether one of the pure and unmixed breed is to be found even in the most remote part of the country from whence, in the first instance, they are supposed to have derived their name. It is affirmed, by the best and most respected authorities, that the Danish-dog, the Irish greyhound and the common greyhound of this country, though they appear so different, are but one and the same race of dog. The Danish-dog, is said by Buffon, to be but a more corpulent Irish greyhound; and that the common greyhound is the Irish greyhound rendered thinner and more fleet by experimental crosses, and more delicate by speculative culture;'

The image by Reinagle, which accompanies the article, flies in the face of the written description as it shows a rough-coated dog, more akin to the Scottish deerhound than the obviously smooth-coated breed described in the text.

The Reverend William Bingley published his, *Memoirs of British Quadrupeds*, in 1809, in which he includes the Irish greyhound, giving a brief description taken from other writers and quoting Lambert in stating there were only eight left, in the hands of the Marquis of Sligo. The accompanying image by Samuel Howitt is of a powerfully built, greyhound with smooth coat.

In 1811, Brightly & Co published, *The Natural History of Quadrupeds and Cetaceous Animals*, which repeated what Oliver Goldsmith had said about the breed, but uses a colourised version of the drawing presented to A.B. Lambert by Lord Altamont as its illustration of the Irish wolfdog.

Irish Greyhound or Wolf Dog. 1809. Engraved by Samuel Howitt for,
Memoirs of British Quadrupeds, by William Bingley.

Irish Wolf Dog. 1811. From, The Natural History of Quadrupeds &
Cetaceous Animals. A colourised version of the Altamont drawing.

Smith & Meyrick in their work, *The Costume of the Original Inhabitants of the British Islands*, of 1815, present two images of the Irish greyhound, one being a chocolate brown dog with some white and the other a white dog pied with black. Both are heavy greyhound types and smooth-coated.

John Christian Curwen, in his, *Observations on the State of Ireland*, published in 1818, made mention of the wolfdog on a visit to Westport House, during the time of the 4th Earl of Altamont.

'This place, some time since, was famous for the Irish wolfdog, which Mr. Pennant supposes was introduced into Ireland by the Danes: I regretted to find that the breed of these dogs had become extinct.'

The death of the last of the Altamont dogs was generally accepted to be when the Irish greyhound became extinct.

Next we have the frontispiece of, Joseph Walker's *Irish Bards, Volume II*, published in 1818, showing an Irish chief with a smooth-coated, Irish greyhound.

Wolfdogs are briefly mentioned by James Stuart in his, *Historical Memoirs of the City of Armagh*, published in 1819.

'Wolves, which were indigenous, and thence styled by the Irish, 'Mac-Tir', – 'son of the earth', have totally disappeared, and, we believe, there is not now a wolf-dog in existence. The late Dr Robinson, (a pupil of the celebrated Boerhave), who lived near Tynan, (in County Armagh), had two immense wolf-dogs, which we have seen accompanying him in the year 1776. These were the last remains of the Ulster wolf-dogs; but Lord Altamont, (since Lord Sligo), had some wolf-dogs, about 20 years ago, at Westport. These are since dead, and the present

Irish Brehons. 1815. From, The Costume of the Original Inhabitants of the British Islands, by Charles Hamilton Smith.

Costume of the Pagan Irish. 1815. From, The Costume of the Original Inhabitants of the British Islands, by Charles Hamilton Smith.

C.Maguire Sc.ʳ

Dublin Pubᵈ by J Christie.

An Irish Chief. 1818. Frontispiece of Irish Bards Volume II,
by Joseph Walker.

Lord Sligo has, we believe, introduced in their stead a kind of double-nosed Grecian water-dogs, larger than Newfoundland dogs; and another species which, in head, resembles a wolf, and in the hinder parts a fox.'

Edward Donovan's, *Natural History of British Quadrupeds, Volume I*, of 1820, contains a colour image of an Irish greyhound showing a white dog pied with black, again, smooth-coated.

In 1846, the *Parliamentary Gazetteer of Ireland* wrote:

'Some of the most remarkable animal remains found at Lagore were those of a very large and powerful dog, apparently of the greyhound tribe, the head measuring in the dry bone nearly eleven inches in length, and characterised by the great extent and magnitude of the crest on the back of the head and the projecting muzzle. In this we have for the first time, an opportunity of judging of the form and character of the Irish wolfdog.'

Irish Greyhound. 1820. From a Natural History of British Quadrupeds, Volume I, by Edward Donovan.

There is an interesting footnote in the historical romance, *The Last Earl of Desmond*, by Charles Bernard Gibson, published in 1854, concerning Irish wolves, which I reproduce here.

'Philip O'Sullivan mentions, in his *'History of the Irish Catholics'*, that after the battle of Kinsale, the hungry wolves hurried from the woods to attack the men who were weak with hunger. There was a native Irish wolf killed at Waringstown, in the county of Down, in the year 1700; and about the same year, a Cormac O'Neill is said, by tradition, to have shot the last of the wolves of Glenshane, in the townland of Sheskinnamaddy, county of Londonderry. The last native wolf of Ireland was seen in the mountains of Kerry, in the year 1720.'

In, *The Zoologist, Volume 20*, (1862), Jonathan Grubb narrates stories told to him by his late father.

'The Wolf-Days of Ireland – My father, whose youth was spent in Ireland, and who died twenty-one years ago, at the age of seventy-four, could tell many very interesting anecdotes, (related to himself by uncles and aunts on his mother's side), connected with the ravages of wolves in that country, in the days when these animals were very formidable there. Some of these accounts are but indistinctly remembered by me; but it was a source of wonder and amusement in early childhood to hear them told by my dear father on a winter's evening. There are one or two very clearly impressed on my memory; and, as the race is now extinct in the British Islands, it may possibly interest the present and coming generations to have them recorded. An ancestor of my father's family led the humble yet pleasant life of a woodcutter, living in a little habitation at some distance from the scene of his labours. He possessed one of those noble and beautiful animals, now also nearly or quite extinct, the Irish wolf-dog, – Turnbull by name, – an almost necessary protection in that day, when a thickly-wooded country afforded abundant shelter for these ferocious masters of the forest, which, even singly, would attack men, and sometimes visit the cottages, and watch their opportunity to carry off young children. Malone, (for I believe that was the man's name), went out to his work one day incautiously unprotected by his faithful dog. He worked later than usual that evening, and towards the close of his day's labour, when he had bound up many fagots of fallen wood, a large and savage wolf issued from the thicker part of the forest and made directly towards him, seeing, no doubt, that he was unarmed and alone. Malone immediately pulled one of the thickest stakes from a bundle of wood and prepared to make the best defence in his power, warding off the attacks of the furious brute, and walking backwards towards home, well knowing that to turn his back to the enemy would be immediately fatal. He also bethought himself that his good friend Turnbull might be just within hearing, and had the presence of mind to call out repeatedly, at the top of his voice, "Turnbull! Turnbull!" Now it so happened that his wife at home felt a little anxious; and the more so, seeing that the dog, instead of being with his master, was lying comfortably asleep before the embers on the hearth. She went out, therefore, to try if she could see or hear anything of her husband, and stood, earnestly watching, on the top of a little hill near the house, when the distant call came upon her ear. In haste she descended, guessing well the nature of the impending danger, and taking the dog to the same spot, she made him stand beside her, gently patting him that he might be still and listen. In a few moments the faithful animal heard – as his mistress had done, and now a little nearer – the well known call, "Turnbull! Turnbull!" No more was needed: the dog instantly darted off at his utmost speed, and was soon lost to the sight of the trembling wife, who gazed after him, riveted, as it were, to the spot where she stood. It need hardly be said how thankful the poor man was to hear his bounding step, nor how quickly the cruel enemy fled on seeing his antagonist approaching. Turnbull, however, followed up the chase, and it was some time before he returned, bearing abundant evidence, in his wounded and blood-stained appearance, what a conflict had taken place between him and the wolf, and leaving little doubt that he had been the victor.

Another case my dear father related, in which a wolf, taking up a little child by his clothes, was carrying it off as fast as such a heavy load would allow him. The child, just old enough to speak, and possibly having been accustomed to be played with, or even thus carried, by one of the large dogs, thought it very nice, and enjoying the ride, exclaimed in the Irish language, "I'm a going!" repeating the words in a singing tone, until rescued from its perilous situation by its parents, who were in time to follow and bring back their darling in safety.

One more instance I remember, in which several wolves attacked one of the Malone family, when returning from a journey on horseback, one dark night. He put spurs to his terrified steed, but the wolves were close behind, and actually made several leaps onto the horse's hindquarters, inflicting severe wounds with their fangs. The traveller just reached his own door, however, himself unhurt, though frightened almost out of his senses, exclaiming to his brother at home, "Oh! James, James, let me in – my horse is ate with the wolves!"

Jonathan Grubb; Sudbury.'

In the *Illustrated Book of the Dog*, of 1881, by Vero Shaw, George A. Graham, (of modern wolfhound fame), gives the following account of the Irish wolfhound.

'Some dogs were owned by the late Hamilton Rowan, of Merrion Square, Dublin, which were erroneously asserted to be Irish wolfhounds. Regarding these dogs the following communication was kindly made to the writer by Mr. Betham, a son of Sir W. Betham before alluded to:

'My father was very intimate with the late Hamilton Rowan, who was the only man possessed of the breed (Irish wolfhound), and who was so chary of it that he would never give away a dog pup without first castrating him. I have repeatedly seen the dogs with him when I was a boy, and heard him tell my father how he became possessed of them. He was in Paris about the time of the first French Revolution, (1789), and was given a dog and a bitch, and was told there that they were *Danish*. He then went to Denmark, thinking he would see more of the breed. When he got there he was told they were not Danish but Irish, and were brought over by someone from Ireland – I forget whom. The dogs were of a very peculiar colour – a kind of brindle blue-and-white, sometimes all brindled and sometimes a great deal of white with large irregular brindle patches, and were much given to weak eyes. They stood about 2 feet 4 or 6 inches at the shoulder, were smooth-haired, and were a most powerful dog. Hamilton Rowan was very proud of being the only possessor of the breed, and seldom went out without one or more accompanying him.'

In a second letter Betham goes on to say:

'I can speak from personal knowledge, and from having often seen the dogs, that the true breed of Irish wolfdogs are smooth-haired, not shaggy like the Scotch deerhound. They were coarse-haired, like the bloodhound. I am not acquainted with the German boarhound (i.e., Great Dane); very possibly they might have been somewhat similar to the Irish breed. Hamilton Rowan's dogs were very powerful, and at the same time active dogs with rather a sharp nose and shrill bark. My father used to say that when he dined at Hamilton Rowan's the dogs used to be in the parlour, and were so tall they could put their heads over the guests' shoulders when sitting at the table, though the dogs were standing on the floor.'

Beyond the shadow of a doubt these dogs were simply Great Danes, as Mr. Rowan had evidently been told in Paris; the description leaves no doubt on that head.'

Despite the fact that Mr. Betham was convinced that Rowan's dogs were genuine Irish wolfdogs, Graham dismisses them as mere Great Danes, mainly I believe, not because they were referred to as Great Danes in France, but because they were smooth-coated, something which did not fit in with his ideas of the Irish hound being a larger, more powerful version of the deerhound. This was a common accusation used by Graham and his cohorts against any dogs in the recent past claiming to be wolfdogs, which were also smooth-coated. They had all, (according to his thinking), been contaminated by Dane blood. It is entirely possible that the dogs in question were Danes or possibly a cross of the Dane with the

Irish wolfdog, but it is of course impossible to say with certainty.

In Rowan's autobiography, published in 1840, (Rowan died in 1834), the Rev. W.H. Drummond wrote:

'His canine favourites were commonly supposed to be of the wolfdog species, but erroneously, as Edward Clibborn Esq., can testify that they were Danish hounds, a keen-scented, quick-running, sheep-killing race, and in other respects very troublesome.'

A further reference to Rowan and his dogs is made by Valentine Lawless, 2nd Baron Cloncurry in his autobiography, *Personal Recollections of the Life and Times'* in 1849.

'Those who remember the streets of Dublin thirty years since, (approx. 1819), can scarcely have forgotten that gigantic old man, in his old-fashioned dress, and with his following of the two last of the race of Irish wolfdogs.'

To which was added a note in his second edition of 1850.

'I have been reminded that Rowan's dogs were of Danish breed, though called by him, and generally supposed to be, Irish wolfdogs. The last existing specimen of the true Irish wolfdog was, I believe, in the possession of the first Marquis of Sligo.' (John Denis Browne, 1756 – 1809)

In conclusion, it is my belief that Rowan's dogs were Irish wolfdogs, though probably with some Great Dane running through them and there is actual photographic evidence to back up this claim. About 1830, Hamilton Rowan gave one of his wolfdogs to Major Jonathan Chetwode of Woodbrook, Portarlington, Co. Laois, who died in 1839. When the dog died in 1833, the head was stuffed and remained at Woodbrook. The Rev. R. Bourke measured the head finding that the length of the head from the tip of the nose to the top of the head was eleven inches, and the width between the ears was five inches. There are two photographs of the head in Hogan's book, one of a side view and the other face on. It is clear that the dog in no way resembles a modern Great Dane; it is less deep throughout with a much less pronounced stop, with much smaller ears, which look to have been erect or semi-erect in life and has none of the loose jowls of the Dane, in fact it appears much more like the head of a powerful, greyhound type of dog. The timescale is against Rowan's dogs being pure Irish wolfdogs but I do believe that the dogs while being classed as Danes by later sources, were composed primarily of the old wolfdog blood. The head in question still exists in the Science and Art Museum in Dublin.

In, *Modern Dogs*, by Rawdon Lee, published in 1893 we have additional information.

'Some four years or so ago, I was shown by the Earl of Antrim a life-sized painting of an enormous hound which had been in his family for about a hundred years. Through generations this had been handed down as a true Irish wolfhound, a noble creature that had saved the life of one of his lordship's ancestors under peculiar and extraordinary circumstances, so the faithful creature had its portrait painted. Now this dog was a huge southern hound in appearance, marked like a modern foxhound, with long, pendulous ears, possibly an animal identical with the matin of old writers. The painting gave the idea that the subject had, in life, stood about thirty-four inches high at the shoulders.'

(The Earl mentioned here was William Randal MacDonnell, the 6th Earl of Antrim, 1851-1918, whose descendants still reside at Glenarm Castle)

This painting is undoubtedly of a scent hound rather than a coursing hound and is far from being a greyhound type of dog as every old writer describes the wolfdog to be. The Earl was mistaken in his belief, quite understandably, as by 1889 the original Irish wolfdog had been extinct for around seventy years. Scent hounds were also used in the wolf hunt to locate and trail the prey until it came within range for the coursing hounds to be slipped, this may account for the error in referring to the dog in the picture as a wolfhound. But, although it may have been used to hunt wolf it most assuredly was not a representative of the breed which had been known as the Irish greyhound or wolfdog.

However, in my research I discovered a portrait of the 2nd Earl of Antrim, (1609-1683), who became the first Marquis of Antrim in 1645. Seated with his hand on the head of what appears to be an Irish wolfdog, so the MacDonnells did have at least an example of the real breed at one time, hence probably the later confusion over the image of the large scent hound. Incidentally this is the same Randal MacDonnell that wrote to Colonel Robert Steuard requesting his 'great dog', quite possibly the same one that appears in the portrait. Lee goes on to say:

'In the museum of the Royal Dublin Society there are two skulls of wolfhounds dug out of barrows by the late Dr Wilde. The dimensions of them have been very useful to those who believed in the bigness of the wolfhound. Unfortunately for the side of the latter, these skulls, when carefully measured and compared with others of living dogs, deerhounds, wolfhounds, and greyhounds, could not have been possessed by animals more than 29 inches high at the shoulders.'

A romantic poem contained in, *The Ballads of Ireland, Volume II* of 1857, portrays the Irish greyhound acting as an avenging spirit, much like the later, *Hound of the Baskervilles*.

CATHAL THE HUNTER
A LEGEND OF LOUGH SWILLY

The hoarse Autumn wind down the valley went sweeping,
    The leaves of the forest hung high on its wing;
The torrents, surcharged, from the mountains came leaping
    To join the fierce raid of the dark Storm-King:
The thunder-clouds burst o'er the breast of Lough Swilly
    The lightning shafts shivered the oaks on its shore;
    And the echoes awakened a fitful reveille,
    And died far away in the hills of Rosscore.

Young Eily sat lone in her ivy-crowned bower,
    For Cathal, the chief, of the dark flowing hair;
But the pulse of her heart had out-counted the hour
    That told of their meeting; no hunter was there:
The big pearly tears on her dark eyelids glisten,
    The throb of her bosom rose loud o'er her breath,
    As she bends by the fast-fading embers to listen,
When the tramp of the charger is heard on the heath

She flies through the night. It roars hoarser and higher
    She hears the deep bay of his dog o'er its swell;
When riderless, foaming, his dark steed sweeps by her –
    The chief that bestrode him lies stretched in the dell!
His last gush of life tinged the foam of the fountain,
    A spear-shaft still drank at the source of its tide;
And his own, that oft pierced the red deer of the mountain,
    Lay shivered, and told that not tamely he died.

A hunter of Eire was Cathal O'Connor:
    The lord of the valley sought Eily O'More;
He sought her in guile, but ere stoop to dishonour,

She wandered a huntress on mountain and shore.
And Cathal, thus doomed, was the friend of her childhood;
And the wand, as the sceptre, had passed from his race:
No castle was his, but a cot by the wild wood,
A wolf-dog, a steed, and a spear for the chase.

The stormwraith, still, through the valley went sighing,
The wolf-dog lay crouched on the rocks at his head,
When the dawning disclosed where the Hunter was lying,
And the bride of his bosom, young Eily was dead!
The death-wail was chaunted, the mourners arrayed them,
And laid them to rest in a cloister so gray;
But the walls of that shrine and the yew-trees that shade them,
Like the race of the island bow down to decay.

The footsteps of Time, down that valley went stealing;
The stag gambolled freely, and drank of its rills;
No music arose from that wood-bosomed sheeling;
No voice of the hunter was heard on the hills;
But often, when midnight in dark spells abounded,
The rock where they weltered, re-echoed their moans,
And the peasants' rough hands raised the Cairn around it,
But their vows of red vengeance outnumbered the stones

The third year had toll'd in that valley of mourning,
Its lord was away at his monarch's behest,
And the bride of his bosom awaits his returning,
Till patience holds war with the fears of her breast:
The deer in the old forest coverts were belling,
And the wraith as before was abroad on the blast;
And the deep midnight bells of the convent were knelling
For souls then departing, and souls that had passed.

Anon, the grey mountains seemed parted asunder;
The owl flapped his wings in the storm fiend's face,
And the lightning-flash leaped from the low-riven thunder,
And convent and castle were rock'd to their base,
All night through the castle, a deathbell kept ringing,
On its turret the raven foreboded of fate;
And a lull in the tempest the dark omen bringing –
Two riderless chargers lay gored at the gate.

The torches were lit. On the round haunted Cairn
The lord lay extended – his spirit had flown;
And his spear that lay fixed, the same night of the year, in
The heart of the Hunter drank deep at his own.
Beside him, in death, lay the page of his training;
Above him a wolf-dog yet dripping with gore,
That glared on the corse with a wild vengeful meaning,
Yelled down through the night and was heard of no more.

And yet in that vale, when the faggot is sparkling,
The tale of the Hunter is told by its light;
And the peasant, abroad, when the shadows are darkling,
Hears strains of wild song, in that valley at night.
And when the full moon of the Autumn breaks o'er him,
A horseman is seen on the hills of Rosscore;
A lady beside, and a wolf-dog before him:
Tis Cathal the Hunter, and Eily O'More.

Mylo

We now jump to recent history and archaeological excavations carried out at Haughey's Fort, County Armagh, in 1987, 1989 and 1991. During these digs three large dog skulls were found. Their lengths were respectively from smallest to largest, 201 mm,

216 mm and 219 mm. This last skull being the largest dog skull ever found in the British Isles up to that point, with an estimated shoulder height of approximately 26 inches. Haughey's Fort is believed to have been occupied from 2200 BC to 800 BC. Were these early examples of Irish greyhounds?

Further excavations carried out at Carrickfergus in County Antrim, between 1991 and 1995, yielded a new record for the largest dog skull unearthed in an archaeological context, at a length of 242 mm. This skull was discovered amongst 14th, 15th and 16th century deposits. Dividing the length of this skull by its width gives a ratio of 1.97. By way of comparison I did the same with several modern breeds with results as follows: greyhound 1.95, Scottish deerhound 2.05, Irish wolfhound 1.99 and Great Dane 1.98. In simple terms, the higher the number, the narrower the skull, the lower the number, the broader the skull. We can see from the results that the Great Dane is the closest match, but that the wolfhound and greyhound are very similar too. Now of course I do not know if the Carrickfergus skull or the modern skulls, (with the exception of the greyhound which was a male), are from males or females. Males typically have broader, stronger skulls than females so this is something to bear in mind. The relevance of this statement is that if the Carrickfergus skull was male or female, it would match better with modern dog breed skulls depending on whether they were male or female. For example, a female greyhound skull might have been a better match for the old skull than the male one used. Nonetheless, the Carrickfergus skull has an estimated shoulder height of approximately 28 inches, a large dog indeed. A very large tibia recovered from the town's 16th/17th century defensive ditch gave an estimated shoulder height of 74.8 cm, almost 29 ½ inches. Breeds which could have produced dogs of this size at this period were very rare, in fact only one comes to mind, the Irish greyhound.

This then concludes my chapter on the history, myth and

legend of the Irish greyhound. Lord Altamont's dogs were generally acknowledged to have been the last surviving remnants of the breed by contemporaries, and these were entirely gone by 1818. Even if we accept Hamilton Rowan's dogs, these seem to have come to an end with his death in 1834.

If we take the rarity of the breed during the seventeenth and eighteenth centuries into account then there is nothing very surprising in this.

One thing for sure is that few breeds of dog have had such a colourful, exciting and romantic history as the Irish greyhound, and when the last example of the breed gave up its final breath, it was inevitable that they would pass into the world of legend.

CHAPTER THREE

ROGUES GALLERY

I thought it might be interesting to compile a list of the personages who are mentioned in the history of the Irish greyhound, well a good few of them anyway. I have provided a thumbnail sketch recording their birth, death, title, and post at the time of their involvement with the Irish greyhound.

Crathlint
King of Scots from 277 to 301. The theft of his favourite hound led to a war between the Scots and the Picts.

Quintus Aurelius Symmachus
Roman Consul in 391. Born 340; died 402. Received seven Irish dogs from his brother Flavinius.

Saint Patrick
Ireland's patron saint. Born 387; died 460. Said to have tended Irish greyhounds on the ship which took him to freedom after his escape from slavery.

Charlemagne/Charles the Great
King of the Franks and Holy Roman Emperor. Born 747; died 814. The earliest version of the, 'Macaire', story takes place in his reign.

Henry II
King of England from 1154 to 1189. Born 1133; died 1189. Travelled to Ireland in 1169, recognised as overlord by Irish kings and received Irish greyhounds as part of an ongoing tribute.

John I
King of England from 1199 to 1216. Born 1166; died 1216. Supposed to have made a gift of the hound Gelert to his son-in-law, Llywelyn, Prince of Wales.

Llywelyn Ab Iorwerth, 'The Great.'
Prince of Wales from 1194 to 1240. Born 1173; died 1240. As tradition has it, the owner of Gelert.

Edward I,
King of England from 1272 to 1307. Born 1239; died 1307. Ordered hounds from Ireland in 1280.

Edward II
King of England 1307 to 1327. Born 1284; died 1327. Had wolfdogs kept for him by William Michell of Wiltshire.

Edward III
King of England from 1327 to 1377. Born 1312; died 1377. Sent his huntsman to retrieve nineteen hounds from Irish lords in 1335.

Charles V 'The Wise.'
King of France from 1364 to 1380. Born 1338; died 1380. The

most popular time period, (1371), for the combat between Aubrie de Montdidier's dog and Macaire to take place.

Henry VIII
King of England from 1509 to 1547. Born 1491; died 1547. Made gifts of Irish greyhounds to a Spanish nobleman.

Thomas Cromwell
Henry VIII's Chief Minister 1532, Master of the Rolls 1534, Lord Privy Seal 1536, Earl of Essex in 1540. Born 1485; died 1540, being beheaded without trial. Philip Roche of Kinsale sent a brace of Irish greyhounds to him in 1535.

Sir Anthony Sentleger
Lord Deputy of Ireland on three occasions. Born 1496; died 1559. Commanded by Henry VIII to supply a Spanish nobleman with Irish greyhounds.

Hernando de Soto
Spanish conquistador who led an expedition into North America. Born 1500; died 1543 on the banks of the Mississippi. He took an Irish greyhound named Bruto with him.

Edward Bellingham
Sir Edward Bellingham, Lord Deputy of Ireland from 1547 to 1548. Born 1506; died 1549. Wrote to James Hancock of Dublin concerning Irish greyhounds.

James Hancock
Mayor of Dublin 1548. Written to by Lord Deputy Bellingham concerning Irish greyhounds.

Edward VI
King of England from 1547 to 1553. Born 1537; died 1553.

Made gifts of Irish greyhounds to a Spanish nobleman, probably a continuation of his father's award.

Shane O'Neill
Ulster chieftain from 1558 to 1567. Born 1530; died 1567. Made a presentation of two Irish greyhounds to Elizabeth I in 1562. Murdered by the MacDonnells' at a feast in Glenshesk.

Brian O'Rourke
Lord of West Breifne from 1566 to 1591. Born 1540; executed for treason 1591. Took four Irish greyhounds with him as a gift when he went to meet James VI of Scotland.

Elizabeth I
Queen of England from 1558 to 1603. Born 1533; died 1603. Received a pair of Irish greyhounds from Shane O'Neill through the Earl of Leicester.

Robert Dudley
Earl of Leicester from 1564 to 1588. Born 1532; died 1588. Go between for Shane O'Neill and Queen Elizabeth I.

Grace O' Malley
The 'Pirate Queen of Mayo'. Born 1530; died 1603. Said to have taken four wolfdogs with her when she went to meet Elizabeth I in London.

Ferdinando I de Medici
Grand Duke of Tuscany from 1587 to 1609. Born 1549; died 1609. Said to have requested Irish greyhounds from the Earl of Essex.

Sir John Perrott
Lord Deputy of Ireland from 1584 to 1588. Born 1527; died

1592. Sent a brace of Irish greyhounds/wolfdogs to Sir Francis Walsingham. Rumoured to have been an illegitimate son of Henry VIII.

Sir Francis Walsingham
Secretary of State from 1573, and Elizabeth I's spymaster. Born 1530; died 1590. Obtained a brace of Irish greyhounds through Sir John Perrott.

Edmund Campion
Distinguished Elizabethan academic, he wrote, *A History of Ireland*, in 1571, in which he mentions the Irish greyhound. Born 1540; executed at Tyburn in 1581.

Richard Stanihurst
Irish historian, mentions Irish greyhounds in the, Ireland, section of *Chronicles of England, Scotland and Ireland*, published by Raphael Holinshed in 1577. Born 1547; died 1618.

William Camden
Historian and scholar. Born 1551; died 1623. Mentioned the Irish greyhound in his work, *Britannia*, of 1586.

Robert Devereux
2nd Earl of Essex from 1576 to 1601. Born 1566; died 1601. Received a request for Irish greyhounds from Henry IV of France and Ferdinando I, Grand Duke of Tuscany. Executed for treason by Elizabeth I in 1601.

Henry IV 'The Great'
King of France from 1589 to 1610. Born 1553; died 1610, (assassinated by a religious fanatic). Henry wrote a letter to the Earl of Essex requesting a pair of Irish greyhounds in 1595.

James VI of Scotland/James I of England
James I of England from 1603 to 1625. Born 1566; died 1625. Received four Irish greyhounds from the Irish noble, Sir Brian O'Rourke.

Peter Lombard
Archbishop of Armagh from 1601 to 1625. Born 1555; died 1625. Described Irish greyhounds as the, 'finest hunting dogs in Europe'.

Lope Felix de Vega Carpio
Spanish playwright. Born 1562; died 1635. He wrote a sonnet about the Irish greyhound.

Sir Arthur Chichester
Lord Deputy of Ireland from 1604 to 1614. Born 1563; died 1625. Sent Irish greyhounds to Viscount Cranbourne and talked of breeding them in a letter of 1605.

Robert Cecil
1st Viscount Cranbourne and 1st Earl Salisbury. Born 1563; died 1612. Received Irish greyhounds from Chichester.

Maurice
Prince of Orange. Born 1567; died 1625. Cecil sent three Irish greyhounds from Ireland to him in 1600.

Fynes Moryson
Secretary to Irish Lord Deputy, Sir Charles Blount, 1600 to 1603. Born 1566; died 1630. Published his, *Itinerary*, in 1617, describing, 'Irish men and greyhounds of great stature.'

Gilbert Talbot
7th Earl of Shrewsbury. Born 1552; died 1616. Acquired Irish

greyhounds from Captain Esmond of Duncannon Fort, County Wexford.

Henry Cary

1st Viscount Falkland; Lord Deputy of Ireland from 1622 to 1629. Born 1576; died 1633. Received a request from the Duke of Buckingham for white Irish greyhounds.

Richard Boyle 'The Great Earl of Cork'

Created 1st Earl of Cork in 1620. Born 1566; died 1643. Extremely influential English settler, with large landholdings in Cork, Waterford, and Tipperary. Appealed to by Viscount Falkland for Irish greyhounds.

Sir Hugh Clotworthy & Lady Marian

Sheriff of County Antrim from 1613 to 1630. Born 1569; died 1630. Married Marian Langford in 1607. A story relates how both wife and castle were saved by a wolfdog.

Christian IV

King of Denmark from 1588 to 1648. Born 1577; died 1648. Given a gift of Irish greyhounds by the Earl of Salisbury.

Sir Thomas Roe

Ambassador to the Court of Emperor Jahangir from 1614 to 1618. Born 1581; died 1644. Requested Irish greyhounds to be presented to Jahangir during his time in India.

Emperor Jahangir

Mogul emperor in India from 1605 to 1627. Born 1569; died 1627. Requested Irish greyhounds from Sir Thomas Roe in 1615.

James Ussher

Anglican Archbishop of Armagh from 1625 to 1656. Born 1581; died 1656. Sent Irish greyhounds to Cardinal Richelieu.

Armand Jean du Plessis

Cardinal Richelieu. Born 1585; died 1642. King Louis XIII's Chief Minister from 1624 to 1642. Received Irish greyhounds from Archbishop Ussher.

Alathea Howard (neé Talbot)

Daughter of Gilbert Talbot. Born 1586; died 1654. Married Thomas Howard, 2nd Earl of Arundel in 1606. She was painted with an Irish greyhound, (most likely a gift from her father), by Peter Paul Rubens in 1620.

Sir Peter Paul Rubens

Flemish artist. Born 1577; died 1640. Painted Alathea Howard with an Irish greyhound.

George Villiers

1st Duke of Buckingham from 1617 to 1628. Born 1592; assassinated 1628. Requested white Irish greyhounds from Lord Deputy Falkland in 1623.

Thomas Wentworth

1st Earl of Strafford and Lord Deputy of Ireland from 1632 to 1640. Born 1593; executed 1641. Wentworth had his portrait painted on two occasions with an Irish greyhound.

Sir Anthony Van Dyck

Flemish portrait painter. Born 1599; died 1641. Painted Wentworth with an Irish greyhound on two occasions.

Giovanni Battista Rinuccini
Roman Catholic Archbishop and Papal Nuncio to Ireland from 1645 to 1649. Born 1592; died 1653. He was given an Irish greyhound whilst in Ireland.

Sir James Ware
Irish antiquarian, M.P., and privy councillor. Born 1594; died 1666. Describes wolfdogs in his work, *Antiquities of Ireland.*

Louis XIII
King of France from 1610 to 1643. Born 1601; died 1643. Sent a gift of six Irish greyhounds in 1623 by James I.

Oliver Cromwell
Lord Protector of England from 1653 to 1658. Born 1599; died 1658. Temporarily owned an Irish greyhound bitch, which was passed on to Dorothy Osbourne.

Henry Cromwell
Son of Oliver Cromwell and Lord Deputy of Ireland from 1657 to 1659. Born 1628; died 1674. Sent a brace of young Irish greyhounds to Dorothy Osbourne.

Dorothy Temple, (neé Osbourne)
Lady Temple, wife of Sir William Temple. Born 1627; died 1695. Made requests for Irish greyhounds to future husband, and Henry Cromwell in 1653, eventually receiving a pair from Cromwell.

Christopher Wase
Schoolmaster and classical scholar. Born 1627; died 1690. Mentions Irish greyhounds in a work of 1654.

John Casimir
King John II of Poland from 1648 to 1668, (abdicated). Born 1609; died 1672. Wase mentions his use of Irish greyhounds in the hunting field.

James Butler
The 12th Earl of Ossory and 1st Duke of Ormonde; Lord Lieutenant of Ireland from 1643 to 1647, 1661 to 1669, and again from 1677 to 1684. Born 1610; died 1688. Requested six Irish greyhounds from his half-brother for his son, the 13th Earl of Ossory.

Thomas Butler
Son of James Butler, and 13th Earl of Ossory. Born 1634; died 1680. Desired to make a gift of two dogs and a bitch each to the King of Spain and the King of Sweden.

Charles II
King of Spain from 1665 to 1700. Born 1661; died 1700. Possibly given Irish greyhounds by the Earl of Ossory.

Charles XI
King of Sweden from 1672 to 1697. Born 1655; died 1697. Possibly given Irish greyhounds by the Earl of Ossory.

Edward Conway
3rd Viscount and 1st Earl Conway. Born 1623; died 1683. Witnessed a dogfight between an Irish greyhound and a mastiff held before King Charles II.

Sir George Rawdon
Managed the Conway estate in Ireland from Lisburn. Born 1604; died 1684. Asked to seek out good Irish wolfdogs by Viscount Conway.

William O'Brien
3rd Earl of Inchiquin from 1692 to 1719. Born 1662; died 1719. Painted with an Irish greyhound by Sir Godfrey Kneller, circa 1685.

Sir Godfrey Kneller
German portrait painter. Born 1646; died 1723. The leading portrait painter of England in his day. Painted William O'Brien with an Irish greyhound.

John Evelyn
English diarist and writer. Born 1620; died 1706. In his famous diary he mentions a dogfight between a mastiff and an Irish greyhound at the Bear Garden in 1669.

John Ray
English naturalist, known as 'the father of British Natural History'. Born 1627; died 1705. He describes the Irish greyhound in 1697 and refers to it as the, 'greatest dog'.

Roderic O' Flaherty
Irish noble and historian, author of, *Iar Connaught* and *Ogygia*. Born 1628; died 1718. Mentions the Irish wolfdog in a tale of Lough Mask.

Sir Heneage Finch
2nd Earl of Winchelsea, Ambassador to Turkey from 1660 to 1669. Born 1628; died 1689. Made a gift of two Irish greyhounds to the Turkish Sultan at Constantinople in 1662.

Cosimo III de Medici
Grand Duke of Tuscany from 1670 to 1723. Born 1642; died 1723. He presented the two Irish greyhounds to Finch, which were subsequently gifted to the Turkish Sultan.

Mehmed IV

Turkish Sultan from 1648 to 1687. Born 1642; died 1693. Presented with a pair of Irish greyhounds by Sir Heneage Finch in 1662. Deposed after his army was defeated by Charles IV, Duke of Lorraine in 1687.

Charles II

King of England from 1660 to 1685. Born 1630; died 1685. Witnessed a dogfight between a mastiff and an Irish wolfdog.

John Dryden

Created first, Poet Laureate, 1668. Born 1631; died 1700. Mentioned Irish greyhounds in one of his poems.

Katherine Philips (Orinda)

English poet who wrote a poem about the Irish greyhound. Born 1631; died of smallpox in 1664.

Patrick Sarsfield

1st Earl of Lucan. Born 1645; died 1693 at the Battle of Landen in Flanders. Said to have been painted with two Irish greyhounds.

Suleiman I

Shah of Persia from 1666 to 1694. Born 1648; died 1694. According to the Reverend Ovington, who had been in Persia, the Shah was presented with a pair of Irish wolfdogs.

Sir Neil O'Neill

2nd Baronet of Shane's Castle and Killyleagh. Born 1658; died from battle wounds 1690. His portrait was painted with an Irish greyhound at his side, by John Michael Wright, in 1680.

John Michael Wright
Scottish portrait painter. Born 1617; died 1694. Painted Sir Neil O'Neill with an Irish greyhound.

John Dunton
English writer and publisher. Born 1659; died 1733. Wrote, *Teague Land, or, A Merry ramble to the Wild Irish* in 1698, in which he mentions a deer hunt with Irish greyhounds.

Sir Murrough Na Mart O'Flaherty
Irish chieftain and grandson of the pirate queen, Grace O' Malley. He was the host who took John Dunton deer coursing with Irish greyhounds.

Johann Elias Ridinger
German natural history artist. Born 1698; died 1767. In 1738 he made an engraving of an Irish greyhound.

Philip Dormer Stanhope
4th Lord Chesterfield and Lord Lieutenant of Ireland from 1745 to 1746. Born 1694; died 1773. Mentions in a letter of 1750 that Irish greyhounds had become extremely rare and hard to get.

Louis Francois de Bourbon
Prince de Conti. Born 1717; died 1776. The French prince that Lord Chesterfield had being trying to acquire Irish greyhounds for.

Carl Linnaeus
An eminent Swedish naturalist known as the, 'Father of Taxonomy'. Born 1707; died 1778. In his classification of dogs he names the Irish greyhound.

Georges-Louis Leclerc

Comte de Buffon and a respected naturalist of his time. Born 1707; died 1788. Refers to the Irish greyhound as the 'chien d'Irlande', and describes the example he has seen.

Thomas Pennant

Welsh naturalist. Born 1726; died 1798. Described the Irish greyhound in his, *British Zoology.*

Oliver Goldsmith

Irish naturalist, playwright, novelist, poet and author of, *An History of the Earth and Animated Nature.* Born 1728; died 1774. He gives a detailed description of the Irish greyhound in his work.

Gabriel Beranger

A Dutch artist who settled in Ireland. Born 1729; died 1817. He describes the Irish greyhound in his journals.

Peter Browne

2nd Earl of Altamont from 1776 to 1780. Born 1731; died 1780. He was painted with an Irish greyhound by Thomas Gibson, circa 1750.

Thomas Gibson

English portrait painter. Born 1680; died 1751. Painted 2nd Earl of Altamont with an Irish greyhound.

Johann Christian Daniel von Schreber

A German naturalist and artist. Born 1739; died 1810. He colourised the engraving by Ridinger of an Irish greyhound in 1785.

George Robert Fitzgerald
The, 'Fighting Fitzgerald', a wealthy landowner, notorious for the number of duels he took part in. Born 1746; died 1786. Shot a wolfdog owned by the 3rd Earl of Altamont. Hanged for murder.

John Denis Browne
The 3rd Earl of Altamont and 1st Marquis of Sligo. Born 1756; died 1809. He lived at Westport House in County Mayo, the last Earl of Altamont to keep Irish greyhounds.

Thomas Bewick
English naturalist and wood-carver. Born 1753; died 1828. Did an excellent woodcut of an Irish greyhound, which appeared in his book, *A General History of Quadrupeds*.

Aylmer Bourke Lambert
English botanist and one of the first fellows of the Linnaen Society. Born 1761; died 1842. Saw Irish greyhounds owned by 3rd Earl Altamont during a visit in 1790.

Maurice Fitzgerald
18th Knight of Kerry. Born 1774; died 1849. Said to have owned Irish wolfdogs at one time.

CHAPTER FOUR

WHAT DID THE IRISH GREYHOUND LOOK LIKE?

Physical Descriptions

This is a question which few people today worry about but, let's examine the evidence. When Graham decided to recreate or revive what he imagined the Irish hound to be, he went down the deerhound route, quite simply he believed that the great wolfdog of Ireland was a larger more powerful version of the Scottish deerhound, (incidentally when I started to write this book my thinking was along those lines too). But, so determined was he to follow his theory that he rejected any evidence from the past which did not support it. Having no agenda as it were myself, I was completely open to any evidence that was available and such evidence as I uncovered I now place before you. I have used only contemporary accounts from the period when Irish greyhounds were generally acknowledged to have existed.

Richardson, the first main proponent of the deerhound link provides very questionable evidence to support his theories and his entire case seems to rest on the belief that until comparatively recently the common greyhound was a shaggy-haired breed. As most of the contemporary accounts of the Irish greyhound or wolfdog compare him closely with the common greyhound this assumption was vital to his case. However, his belief does not stand up to scrutiny. When searching for descriptions of the common greyhound of the same period when the wolfdog existed I found the following accounts.

1406-1413. *The Master of Game*, by Edward, Duke of York.

'Allan gentil: is like a grayhound in all properties and parts, his thicke and short head excepted.'

(The three varieties of allan or alaunt described were all smooth-coated).

1570. *De Cannibus Britannicus*, by Johannes Caius, (Dr John Kaye)

'…some are of a greater sorte, and some of a lesser, some are smooth skinned, and some are curled,'

(Referring to greyhounds)

1866. In G.R. Jesse's work we have the following reference to sport in 1671.

'In the 'Severall wayes of Hunting, Hawking & Fishing', according to the English manner, invented by Francis Barlow, and Etched by W. Hollar in 1671; both fox, stag, otter, and hare hunting are portrayed. The dogs are slow, heavy, flap-eared hounds. Red Deer are coursed with large smooth greyhounds, and spaniels are used in hawking.'

1675. *The Gentleman's Recreation*, by Nicholas Cox.

'Likewise he must have long legs, thin and soft hairs.'

1749-1788 *Natural History*, by Buffon.

'The large Dane, the Irish greyhound, and the common greyhound, though they appear different at the first sight, are nevertheless the same dog; the large Dane is no more than a plump Irish greyhound; and the common greyhound is only the Irish greyhound, rendered more thin and delicate by care.'

(Great Danes have never been anything other than a smooth-coated breed).

Undoubtedly there were shaggy-coated greyhounds as there are references and images indicating such, but the majority of references and images have been of the smooth-coated variety.

Another blow to Richardson's and the later Graham's case can be found in a chapter on the Scotch greyhound, contained in Brown's, *Anecdotes of Dogs*, published in 1829.

'This dog, in point of form, is similar in all respects to the common greyhound, differing only in its being of a larger size, and in the hair being wiry, in place of that beautiful sleekness which distinguishes the coat of the other. Their colour for the most part is of a reddish-brown, or sandy hue, although they are sometimes to be met with quite black. I saw some animals of this description in the north of Ireland, in possession of the small farmers and peasants of the mountainous districts. They are said to be the only dogs which are capable of catching the hares which inhabit these mountain ranges, – the common greyhound wanting strength for such a laborious chase. These dogs in Ireland are almost universally dark iron grey, with very strong grizzly hair, and are much superior in many respects to any I have seen in Scotland. I remarked a peculiarity in those Irish hounds, which was that of having very small but extremely brilliant and penetrating hazel-coloured eyes; their teeth were also very strong and long.'

From this it would appear that the Scotch greyhound was found in both Scotland and Ulster and that the two populations were classed as the same breed, for Richardson and Graham, so far so good. This is not surprising as there have been centuries old connections between Ulster and the west of Scotland. But, it is especially interesting to note that no one who owned the breed either in Ireland or Scotland claimed them to be Irish wolfdogs, Brown himself was in no doubt that the wolfdog was a smooth-coated breed.

'In shape the Irish Greyhound somewhat resembles the common greyhound, only that he is much larger, and more muscular in his formation,'

When we direct our attention to descriptions of the Irish greyhound or wolfdog we find the following accounts.

1571. Edmund Campion who wrote, *A History of Ireland.*

'The Irish are not without wolves and greyhounds to hunt them, bigger of bone and limb than a colt.'

1577. Richard Stanihurst repeats the above description word for word in Holinshed's, *Chronicles of England, Scotland and Ireland.*

1585. Sir John Perrott, Lord Deputy of Ireland.

'…a brace of good wolfdogs, one black, one white.'

1586. Camden, in his, *Britannia.*

'The Irish wolfhound is similar in shape to a greyhound,
bigger than a mastiff, and tractable as a spaniel.'

1596. Lope de Vega.

'An Irish greyhound of beauteous build,
Bay-coloured, dark-striped from head to haunch,' (Brindle)

1601. Moryson, Secretary to the Lord Deputy of Ireland.

'The Irish men and greyhounds are of great stature.'

1615. Rev. Edward Terry.

'Large Irish greyhounds…great Irish greyhounds'

1617. Sir Thomas Roe on behalf of Emperor Jahangir.

'…tall Irish greyhounds'

1623. Viscount Falkland, Lord Deputy of Ireland to the Earl of Cork.

'And, if you can possibly, let them be white, which is the
colour most in request here.'

1632. Randle Cotgrave.

'An Irish greyhound, a great greyhound.'

1646. Rinuccini, Papal Nuncio to Ireland.

'…which by his majesty, great size, the marvellous variegation of his colour, (pied), and the proportion of his limbs…'

1652. Oliver Cromwell.

'…such great dogges, as are commonly called wolfe dogges'

1654. Sir James Ware in his, *Antiquities of Ireland*.

'…they are endowed with extraordinary strength, size and beauty.'

1662. Grand Duke Cosmo III.

'…two large and comely Irish greyhounds.'

1669. *The Diary of John Evelyn*.

'…the Irish wolfdog exceeded, which was a tall greyhound,'

1675. Nicholas Cox in, *The Gentleman's Recreation*.

'Some dogs are very great, as the wolfdog, which is shaped like a greyhound, but by much taller, longer and thicker;…The best greyhound hath a long body, strong and reasonably great, not so big as the wolfdog in Ireland.'

1697. John Ray, the naturalist.

'The greatest dog I have yet seen, surpassing in size even the mollossus, (mastiff), as regards shape of body and general character similar in all respects to the common greyhound; their use is to catch wolves.'

1748. Harris.

'The English mastiff was in no way comparable to the Irish wolfdog in size and shape.'

1750. Lord Chesterfield.

'...large dogs of Ireland.'

1772. Brooke, in, *Natural History*.

'The Irish wolfdog is, as 'Ray', affirms, the highest dog he had ever seen, being much larger than a mastiff dog but more like a greyhound in shape.'

1774. Oliver Goldsmith in, *Animated Nature*.

'The largest of those I have seen, and I have seen above a dozen, was about four feet high, or as tall as a calf of a year old. He was made extremely like a greyhound, but rather more robust, and inclining to the figure of the French matin, or the Great Dane. His eye was mild, his colour white, and his nature seemed heavy and phlegmatic... the Irish wolfdog, whose ears resemble those of the greyhound.'

1774. Charles Smith in his, *History of Waterford*.

'This dog is much taller than the mastiff, but made more like a
greyhound...'

1775. Richard Twiss, *A Tour in Ireland.*

'...they were much taller than a mastiff, or than any dog I had
seen, and appeared to be of great strength. Their shape was
somewhat like that of a greyhound;'

1775. Buffon in his, *Natural History.*

'I never saw but one of them, and he appeared as he sat to be
about five feet high, and in form resembled the large Danish
dog; but exceeded him very much in his size. He was quite
white, and his manner was perfectly gentle and peaceable...
The Irish greyhound, the large Dane, and the common
greyhound, have, besides the resemblance of form and long
snout, the same dispositions;'

1777. Thomas Pennant in, *British Zoology.*

'I have seen two or three in the whole island: they were of the
kind called by M. de Buffon, Le grand Danois,'

1779. The artist, Gabriel Beranger.

'They are amazing large, white, with black spots, but of the
make and shape of the greyhound, only the head and neck
somewhat larger in proportion.'

1789. Gough in his edition of, *Camden.*

'...are generally about three feet high, sometimes larger; white,
or white with a few black or brown spots.'

1790. Thomas Bewick in, *General History of Quadrupeds*.

'The Irish greyhound is the largest of the dog kind…These dogs
are about three feet high, generally of a white or cinnamon
colour, somewhat like a greyhound, but more robust.'

1790. Aylmer Bourke Lambert.

'…from the toe of the foreleg to the top of the shoulders,
28 ½ in….The hair, short and smooth; the colour, brown
and white of some, others black and white. They seem good-
natured animals, but, from the account I received, are now
degenerated in size, having been larger some years ago, and
their make more like a greyhound.'

1803. William Taplin in, *The Sportsman's Cabinet*.

'It is affirmed, by the best and most respected authorities,
that the Danish-dog, the Irish greyhound and the common
greyhound of this country, though they appear so different,
are but one and the same race of dog. The Danish-dog, is said
by Buffon, to be but a more corpulent Irish greyhound; and
that the common greyhound is the Irish greyhound rendered
thinner and more fleet by experimental crosses, and more
delicate by speculative culture;'

1809. Rev. William Bingley in his, *Memoirs of British Quadrupeds*.

'The Irish greyhound is supposed to be the largest of all the
dog kind as well as one of the most beautiful and majestic in
its appearance. Its limbs are proportionally more stout and
strong; and its whole formation much heavier than that of the
common greyhound.'

1811. *The Natural History of Quadrupeds and Cetaceous Animals.* This is composed of the works of many naturalists, with the section on the Irish greyhound being a copy of Goldsmith's writings.

1820. *The Natural History of British Quadrupeds,* by Donovan, gives a very brief account of the Irish greyhound.

'Size of the common mastiff: this dog is now become very rare.'

These then are the written accounts from which to generate a description of the Irish greyhound, so what can we say with confidence?

Size. It was a large dog, the tallest dog then living. Larger than a mastiff, which in those days, according to Goldsmith, averaged around 24 inches at the shoulders, (they were a smaller, much more athletic breed in those days and a good deal healthier). So, the height of an Irish greyhound would most likely have been from 28 inches up, at the shoulders. Lambert measured one of the last at 28 ½ inches, but the owner stated they were much reduced in size from what they had been formerly.

Type. They were of a distinctly greyhound type. Repeatedly described as being like very large greyhounds, but with heavier bone, stronger heads, heavier necks and more powerful throughout.

Coat. Resembling the common greyhound and the Great Dane, both smooth-coated breeds, the coat is also described as short and smooth.

Colour. Clearly described in the text as being available in the following colours; black, white, black and white, brown and white, cinnamon or brindle. I think it a fair assumption to say that the breed probably came in the same colours as the common greyhound, the two breeds being similar in so many other ways.

The Irish Greyhound in Art

Of course another way of finding out what the Irish greyhound looked like is to simply find images of them. However, this is not as easy as one would imagine, there are said to be only two genuine likenesses of the breed, portraits by two German artists, Johann Elias Ridinger and Johann Christian Dan Schreber.

I was certain however, that other paintings of, or containing Irish greyhounds do exist, when we look at the people who owned them, they were the very cream of Europe and further afield; emperors, kings, czars, queens, princes, counts, dukes, earls, lords and ladies, in short, the richest, most powerful people in the world. These were people who flaunted their wealth and position, they built magnificent houses, filled with treasures, they had portraits painted of themselves in their finery and they prided themselves in the quality of their horses, hunting dogs, hawks and fighting cocks. Therefore, I would find it inconceivable, that none of them would have had such an exclusive and valuable possession like an Irish greyhound recorded in paint.

Indeed, I have managed to find other images of the Irish greyhound during the time period when they are believed to have existed, that is, up to 1820. I think 1820 is as late as I would care to go for accurate artistic representations of the Irish greyhound. We know the Altamont dogs were gone before 1818 and they were generally accepted to be the last of the wolfdogs and even the dogs of Hamilton Rowan appear to have ended with his death in 1834. As in the written descriptions I will go through the images in chronological order.

The first image is, *'Charles V with a Hound'*, by Titian, painted in 1533. Charles V became King of Spain in 1516 and Holy Roman Emperor in 1519 and the dog in the picture is thought to have been a favourite. The dog itself is a very tall, greyhound type, but with a much stronger head, indeed very much like the written accounts describing the Irish greyhound or wolfdog. To have been included in such a portrait a dog would necessarily have been highly bred or valuable and none were more so than the Irish greyhound at this time, also it is simply too big to have been anything else. There is also a suit of armour for a greyhound type dog in the Museum of Armoury, Madrid, dated between 1530 and 1540 and made by Desiderius Helmschmid as a special commission from Charles V. The dog in question much have been highly regarded by the king as the cost of the armour would have been great. The armour was also engraved with the scene of a man standing ready with spear to receive the charge of a wild boar, which indicates that the dog wearing the armour would have been used in this way. As the painting by Titian dates to 1533 I think it likely that the armour was made for the dog pictured with the king.

Next, we diverge into sculpture and the, *'Masserene wolfhound'* of Antrim Castle, circa 1612. It is my belief that this sculpture was probably commissioned by Sir Hugh Clotworthy as a present for his wife, Lady Marian following her rescue from the wolf by an Irish greyhound. I have inspected the sculpture myself and it is certainly no work of art being very crude, probably the work of an amateur mason. But, crude though it is a few points can be garnered from it; the dog has a long muzzle, a characteristic of greyhound breeds, its ears are fairly small and droop, like those of a greyhound, it is powerfully built, much more so than a normal greyhound, it is smooth-coated, there is no sign of an attempt at showing rough or long hair and lastly, it could be ferocious as indicated by its bared teeth. Taking all these points in, there is no doubt in my mind that the sculptor was trying to portray an Irish greyhound of the period.

The third image is a painting of Alathea Howard, the Countess of Arundel together with Sir Dudley Carleton, attendants, and with her hand upon its head, an Irish greyhound. Dated to 1620 and painted by no less than Rubens, it exactly embodies the written descriptions we have of the breed. The Countess was the daughter of Gilbert Talbot who received Irish greyhounds in 1608, eliminating any doubt as to the breed of dog in the painting. I had discovered the image on a greyhound website and realised the dog was no ordinary greyhound and then several months later came across a reference to it during further research in an article on the Irish wolfhound by James Watson in his, *The Dog Book*, published in 1905, in which, referring to the painting, he says,

'The size of the dog is much greater than the greyhounds of that period and we infer that it is an Irish wolfdog.'

Again from Europe there is a portrait by Van Dyck of Wolfgang Wilhelm, Count Palatine of Neuburg, accompanied by a huge, greyhound type dog, dating to circa 1628. The breed of dog is not named but with its physical characteristics it could only be an Irish greyhound or a forerunner of the breed which would become known as the Great Dane.

Next there are two portraits of Thomas Wentworth, the Earl of Strafford by Van Dyck. The first image dates from 1633 and the second 1639, and in both the Earl is accompanied by a white Irish greyhound, which appears to be the same dog. Why am I so certain as to the breed? Well, the dogs are very large, greyhound type animals so they couldn't be anything else and both paintings were done during his time as Lord Deputy of Ireland where he would be very well placed to acquire them.

Alathea Howard, Countess Arundel. 1620. Sir Peter Paul Rubens.
Bavarian State Painting Collections – Alte Pinakothek Munich.

Wolfgang Wilhelm, Count Palatine & Duke of Neuberg. 1628.
Van Dyck.

Thomas Wentworth, Earl of Strafford. 1639. Van Dyck. From the collection of Lady Juliet Tadgell.

175

In Ware's *Antiquities*, (1654), the frontispiece shows 'Hibernia' holding the leash of a couple of smooth greyhounds. The rest of the picture seems to be displaying Ireland's bounty in the form of cattle, sheep, wildfowl in the air, bees with a hive in a tree, water indicated by a meandering river, abundant woodland and plentiful deer. It therefore makes sense that the greyhounds in the etching would also be from Ireland and thus examples of the Irish greyhounds mentioned by Ware. Their relatively ordinary size can be explained by the fact that artists through the ages who depicted gods or national symbols, have for the most part portrayed them in superhuman size.

I have also found a painting of the 1st Marquis of Antrim in formal pose with one hand on the head of a large, white-headed dog, which could only be an Irish greyhound. Could this be the dog he wrote to his cousin about in 1656?

In an article by Edward C. Ash, which appeared in, *The American Kennel Gazette* of October 1938, we find another interesting image with the following comments:

'I can hardly end this short note on the breed without saying that I happened to discover an illustration of the very time that the breed was the most famous, when the British Government was importing the breed. It is marked 'Irish greyhound' so that there can be no doubt as to its type and the illustration shows a dog somewhat like a Great Dane, a smooth-skinned animal, suggesting that the Irish dogs had not, necessarily, a wire rough and hard coat, though, of course, some may have had so.'

The illustration is a lively one portraying an athletic greyhound type dog with a strong head, dated to 1665. Ash had used the same image in his, *Practical Dog Book* of 1931 and tells us it was found in an old book in the British Museum but unfortunately doesn't provide the title, but I do believe it to be genuine. He again uses this image in his, *Book of the Greyhound*, together with a second image of an Irish wolfdog killing a wildcat, dated to 1671 by Francis Barlow. Again, this second image shows a powerful, smooth-coated greyhound type dog.

Probably the image I was most excited to find was a portrait of Sir Neil O'Neill, 2nd Baronet of Shane's Castle and Killyleagh, by John Michael Wright, dated to 1680.

O'Neill stands proud in full Irish chieftain regalia whilst on his left a huge, brown and white Irish greyhound stands gazing up at his face. The dog is greyhound in type but looks immensely powerful.

The sitter in the next portrait was William O'Brien, 3rd Earl of Inchiquin, painted by Sir Godfrey Kneller, circa 1685. O'Brien is suitably posed whilst his right hand rests on the neck of a large, smooth-coated dog, undoubtedly an Irish greyhound as he was known to have the breed, having given two of them to Rev. Ovington when he landed at Kinsale.

There is an interesting painting, circa 1720s, of John Campbell, Lord Glenorchy, later to become the 3rd Earl of Breadalbane. It shows him standing in a typically, fairly camp pose of the time with a huge, powerful, greyhound type dog alongside. The dog is smooth-coated and black and white in colour and I believe it is most likely an Irish greyhound or at least contains Irish greyhound blood.

The year, 1738, brings us to the first of only two images which were accepted up till now as being of original Irish wolfdogs, and that is the engraving by the German naturalist Ridinger. It is entitled, 'large Irish greyhound,' and shows a greyhound type dog with snipey muzzle, which appears to be white, pied with a darker colour and smooth-coated.

Another portrait thought to be by Thomas Gibson, and dating to circa 1750, shows Peter Browne, the 2nd Earl of Altamont, (a family famously associated with the breed), standing in formal pose

Sir Neil O' Neill. 1680. John Michael Wright. Photo Tate.

John Campbell, Lord Glenorchy. 1720s'. Enoch Seeman. Photo Philip Mould Ltd, London/Bridgeman Images.

with one hand on the head of a devoted looking, large, powerful, smooth-coated, greyhound type dog, which in the title of the painting is referred to as an Irish wolfhound. Thus, eliminating any doubt about the breed concerned.

The second, generally accepted image till now was a painting by the naturalist Schreber contained in a work of 1774. It shows a white dog with tan patches, but it is nothing more than a colour version of Ridinger's engraving.

There is an image of an Irish greyhound in Buffon's, *Natural History*, of 1775, but it is merely a reversed image of 'le matin' dog from the same work and contradicts his written description, so I place no value in it.

In 1790 we have the woodcut by Thomas Bewick of an Irish greyhound, thought to be of one of Lord Altamont's dogs. These were discredited by later writers as having Great Dane blood, without any proof, mainly it would seem because the dogs were smooth-coated, (these were the writers who favoured the deerhound link). But, I have to say the Bewick woodcut certainly meets the written descriptions of the Irish greyhound.

Again, dated to 1790, there is also the Lord Altamont drawing, presented to A.B. Lambert, depicting what he referred to as a mastiff wolfdog, it is a heavy looking animal which to me indicates a cross or at least a deterioration in the breed, which indeed is very likely as they were near the end at this time. Though again, the dog appears to be white with patches of colour and smooth-coated.

William Taplin's, *The Sportsman's Cabinet*, of 1803, deals with the Irish greyhound and an image is provided by Reinagle of a rough-coated, deerhound type dog whose face is curiously turned away from the reader, but as the image is completely at odds with the written text, and is most likely an imagined dog, I place no value in it.

In 1809 we have the 'Irish greyhound or wolf-dog' plate by Howitt, portrayed in Rev. William Bingley's, *Memoirs of British*

Quadrupeds. The Bingley dog is again smooth-coated and a powerful greyhound type of animal.

The Natural History of Quadrupeds and Cetaceous Animals, published in 1811 repeats what Oliver Goldsmith said about the breed, but uses the image presented to A.B. Lambert by Lord Altamont to illustrate the Irish wolfdog, albeit now in a colourised form, showing a white dog pied with black.

The artist, Charles Hamilton Smith, depicts Irish greyhounds twice in, *The Costume of the Original Inhabitants of the British Islands,* a book published in 1815. One dog is white, pied with black and the other a chocolate brown and white. Both dogs are large, greyhound in type and smooth-coated.

Next we have the frontispiece of, *Irish Bards, Volume II,* by Joseph Walker, published in 1818, showing an Irish chief with a smooth-coated, Irish greyhound.

The last image I have been able to find before my self-imposed cut-off date of 1820, is in Edward Donovan's, *Natural History of British Quadrupeds, Volume I,* of that year. There is a colour image of an Irish greyhound showing a white dog pied with black, again, smooth-coated.

So, what can we say about the Irish greyhound from these representations in art?

Size. It is impossible to give any accurate indication of size from the pictures except to say that the dogs in the paintings of Countess Arundel, the Earl of Strafford and Sir Neil O'Neill, do appear to be of considerable stature.

Type. There is no doubt that all the dogs are greyhound in type, though more powerful throughout, with heavier bone, and stronger heads, and necks.

Coat. All the dogs without exception are smooth-coated.

Colour. It is impossible to say with certainty the colour of the dogs portrayed in black and white, but the colour representations by Rubens, Van Dyck and Wright speak for themselves; Rubens portrays a white dog pied with black on the head and body, Van Dyck a white dog, and Wright, a red fawn dog with white markings.

CHRONOLOGY OF IMAGES

Date	Images
1533	*Charles V with a Hound, by Titian*
1612	*Statue of Antrim wolfdog created*
1620	*Alathea Howard, Countess Arundel by Sir Peter Paul Rubens*
1628	*Wolfgang Wilhelm, Count Palatine and Duke of Neuburg painting, by Van Dyck*
1633	*Thomas Wentworth, Earl of Strafford by Van Dyck*
1639	*Thomas Wentworth, Earl of Strafford by Van Dyck, 2nd portrait*
1654	*Frontispiece to Sir James Ware's Antiquities of Ireland*
1657?	*Randal MacDonnell, 1st Marquis of Antrim*
1665	*The, Irish Greyhound, artist unknown*
1671	*The Irish wolfdog by Francis Barlow*

1680   Sir Neil O'Neill, by John Michael Wright

1685   William O'Brien, 3rd Earl of Inchiquin by Sir Godfrey
       Kneller

1720s John Campbell, Lord Glenorchy by Enoch Seeman

1738   Gross Irlandisch Windspiel, (large Irish greyhound) by
       Ridinger

1750? Peter Browne, 2nd Earl of Altamont by Thomas Gibson

1774   Canis Familiaris, (Irish greyhound) by Schreber

1790   The, Irish Greyhound, by Thomas Bewick

1790   The Altamont, Irish Wolfdog, presented to A.B. Lambert

1809   The, Irish Wolfdog, by Howitt, in Bingley's Quadrupeds

1811   The Natural History of Quadrupeds and Cetaceous Animals,
       a colour version of the Altamont drawing

1815   Charles Smith depicts Irish greyhounds twice in, The
       Costume of the Original Inhabitants of the British Islands

1818   The frontispiece of Walker's, Irish Bards, Volume II,
       shows an Irish chief with a smooth-coated Irish greyhound

1820   Edward Donovan's, Natural History of British Quadrupeds,
       Volume I, Plate XXII, Irish greyhound'

By 1818, the last of the Altamont Irish wolfdogs were dead,

Irish greyhound/wolfdog, as depicted on the sixpence of the Republic of Ireland, 1928. One of eight designs submitted by Percy Metcalfe which were first issued 12th December 1928.

these were considered the last of the pure breed, though as I have previously stated it is my belief they had already been crossed. Hamilton Rowan's dogs were gone with his death in 1834 and although dismissed as Great Danes by contemporaries I do believe they contained Irish greyhound blood.

CHAPTER FIVE

WHAT WERE THEY USED FOR?

Hunting, Guarding and Warfare

Historically the Irish greyhound could be used for three things, hunting, guard work and war. So, exactly what did this entail? Well, let us have a hoke around, (as we say in Ulster), and see what we can find.

A Guard/War Dog's Role

Although there are still war-dogs around today, their role is somewhat different from the canines of the past. The modern army has 'sniffer' dogs used to detect explosives, contraband, and to track people, a variety of breeds are used such as, springer spaniels, Labradors and Alsatians. But they also have attack trained war-dogs to protect military compounds, their job is to apprehend intruders and give warning of attack. This used to almost exclusively be the job of the Alsatian, or German shepherd, a breed found to give a good combination of strength, athleticism, intelligence and manageability, but due to poor breeding practices caused by the show ring they have largely been replaced today by the Malanois, a very similar type of dog but without the physical defects. The Malanois also seems to be the dog of choice for use in Special Forces operations to detect explosives, weaponry and enemy personnel, even engaging them. But, as regards full scale battle, dogs just aren't used.

However, prior to the invention of firearms, dogs could take an active part in the battle itself. This was the case from the earliest times and was a natural thing for the dog to do, as part of its human pack, a dog would fight alongside the other pack members against any rival pack, just as a wolf pack will fight a rival pack to defend its territory. The breeds of dog used in this way varied according to locality, the first requisite was courage, the dog had to be willing to attack an armed man and indeed continue the attack even if badly wounded, the second was strength, the more powerful the dog the more damage it was capable of inflicting and as strength naturally went with size, the larger canines were favoured. The ancients found these qualities in the large flock guarding dogs, such as the molossus, the large coursing hounds and most of all in the mastiff breeds. It is no accident that these were the breeds used to contending against large and dangerous game, a dog that will attack a raging boar or bear will certainly have courage enough for a man.

That the molossus, (which seems to have resembled a larger, more powerful German shepherd), and the mastiff types were used as war-dogs is no surprise, but coursing hounds do at first seem to sit a little uncomfortably in this group. However, the larger coursing hounds have been used since earliest times to bring down big game such as red deer. To give the reader a modern comparison let us look at the Scottish deerhound, the largest of today's true coursing hounds, here we have an animal which can be 30 inches plus at the shoulders and weigh over 105 lbs, a dog used in the past to bring down the formidable red stag and incidentally is still used today in various parts of the world to hunt deer and coyote. Given the inclination, how would a dog like this cope with your average adult male, the answer, very, very, easily!

The people friendly temperament of today's greyhounds and deerhounds is probably responsible for this mindset, one just doesn't see them as being aggressive, but, imagine if you will, a deerhound of the size stated, attacking you with the same intensity he would attack a deer; 105 lbs of muscle, bone and sinew coming behind a large set of fangs with the intention of doing you the maximum possible damage; a sobering thought I think you will agree! And the coursing hound being used as a war-dog came into its own, right here in Ireland with the evolution of the most formidable coursing hound ever to have existed, the Irish greyhound.

So, exactly what was the war-dog's role on the early battlefields of Ireland? To understand this we first need to look at a contemporary army. An army of the pagan/early Christian period could range from a few dozen for an inter-tribal spat, to hundreds, (I would think rarely thousands), for a province v province battle. They would be armed mostly with spear and shield, or the occasional axe, and a sword for the wealthier chieftains, there would be little in the way of body armour and the combatants would mostly have been infantry. Some of the wealthier participants would have fought from horseback, using spears or long swords, or from chariots by throwing javelins before descending to fight on foot. Boys could have been used as auxiliaries in the form of slingers. Into this scenario we introduce the Irish greyhound; we have already discovered that in legend and in fact, the head of the army was also in charge of the king's hounds, this would indicate a close involvement between the two and perhaps a role in battle for the hounds. My belief is that the dogs, some of which may have been trained up for battle, were used to attack the enemy cavalry and chariots, both man and horse, and the more lightly armed auxiliaries such as slingers and archers. Let us examine the effect of an attack on each; a pack of large, ferocious dogs attacking cavalry could have been devastating, both horse and man would be attacked, riders pulled from the saddle, horses pulled down, others thrown into blind panic and bolting, being impossible to control; suffice to say, a cavalry attack could be completely nullified by the use of war-dogs, and this could decide the outcome of a battle. Chariots too, would have been easy prey, with the horses attacked and indeed the charioteer getting an extra passenger in the form of something large and ferocious with teeth! Slingers or archers with no other protection and on foot would have been torn to pieces by the war-dogs. I think it most likely that the dogs would have been used to target enemy cavalry and chariots, and of course there was the matter of the dogs belonging to the opposing force, so the army with more or better war-dogs had a lot to gain, whichever side won the battle of the war-dogs had a tremendous advantage in the rest of the battle. With victory gained and one side in retreat, the war-dogs again could prove a devastating tool. Warriors fleeing for their lives, many wounded, casting aside shields and weapons to run more quickly, would have proved easy prey for the great wolfdog and carnage would have resulted. There are stories of the Irish greyhound decapitating warriors, some may dismiss this as fanciful, but there are historical records written by conquistadors who threw live Indians to their war-dogs with just such a result.

Looking further afield we have references to the use of dogs in battle from various sources. From a chest found in the tomb of Tutankhamun (r.1333-1324 BC), we have depictions of mastiffs in the full midst of battle attacking Nubian warriors with deadly effect.

Polyaenus, in his, *Strategems*, circa 163 AD, recounts how King

Alyattes of Lydia (r.610-560 BC), used dogs to repel an invading army of Cimmerian cavalry.

'...fell upon the barbarians, as they would on a heard of wild beasts; tore many of them, so as to disable them and put them from action and put others to flight shamefully.'

An interesting account of how dogs were used in battle comes to us from Aelian (170- 230 AD) in his, *De Natura Animalium*, in which he describes how the Magnesians utilised their canines.

'Each of the cavalry took as his companion on campaign a hunting dog and a slave javelin thrower. When battle was due to begin the dogs, which were fearsome, aggressive and ferocious to encounter; rushed forward and disturbed the enemy formation; the slaves jumped out in front of their masters and threw javelins. After the disorder already caused by the dogs, the activity of the slaves also had its effect. Finally in their place the masters attacked.'

According to Pliny the Elder, in his, *Natural History*, the King of the Garamantes in North Africa was

'...led back from exile by 200 dogs who fought those trying to oppose him.'

The way in which dogs could be successfully employed against cavalry is described by Olaf Mansson, (Olaus Magnus), in his work of 1555, *A History of the Northern Peoples*, under a chapter titled, *On the different ways in which Finns fight battles.*

'No less support is given to these Finns by their huge, snapping dogs, since the horses of the Russians fear and flee these as much as the Persian horses do camels. These dogs attack the nostrils of the horses, as they have been trained to do, by leaping up and biting them. Hence in their terror the horses suddenly rear up on their hind legs and throw their riders to die there and then or to be taken prisoner.'

So, we can say that Irish greyhounds were highly valued as war-dogs that took an active role in battle and as such they were an integral part of armies in Ireland up to the Middle Ages. Well..., actually no. As I found in my research, by far the primary use for the Irish greyhound was as a hunting dog, it is true they also made formidable personal protection dogs, but regular large scale use on the battlefield? There just isn't any concrete evidence to support this. Now, there is no argument that a large force of Irish greyhounds would have been an asset to any army, (especially pre-firearms), but there is also a major problem. There were no professional standing armies at this time, armies were only formed up when a campaign or battle was to be waged. Essentially you could have an army gathered from around the province that were literally strangers to each other and more importantly to the dogs. So when the time for battle arrived and the dogs were loosed they could as likely attack friend as foe, especially after both sides collided and the fog of war descended. This of course could prove disastrous and would seem to me to be why the Irish greyhound's, (or any breed's use), as a war-dog would be very limited.

Hunting in Ireland

As we have already learnt in a previous chapter, the Irish greyhound was regarded as a supreme hunting dog, and the hunting field rather than the battlefield would have been his primary calling. So what animals made up his quarry? If we go back to the great hound's heyday there was a good variety of game on which to test its mettle, so let us analyse each quarry in turn and see just what he had to cope with.

Rabbit

Oryctolagus cuniculus
Length – 40cm
Weight – 1.2 to 2kg
The humble rabbit is probably the most commonly coursed animal in Britain and Ireland today. It is not a native to Ireland, like the fallow deer it was introduced by the Normans. The first reference to them in Ireland is a charter granted to Hugh de Lacy in Connaught in 1204 giving him permission to establish warrens. It is doubtful that the rabbit was ever a common quarry for the Irish greyhound, rabbits are never far from cover and are very agile. A dog the size of the Irish greyhound is just not made to course rabbits.

Qualities Required:
Speed
Agility

Irish Hare

Lepus timidus hibernicus
Length – 52 to 58cm
Weight – 2.5 to 3.5kg
A somewhat smaller cousin of the brown hare, the Irish hare is very fast and agile, with stamina enough to tax the fittest of dogs. It always seems to have been regarded as a sporting animal rather than a food item, with the course itself being the object of the sport. Few Irish greyhounds would have been used to course hares, the very large dogs would just have been too clumsy to put in a decent show, but the smaller animals of the 28 to 30 inch range I believe would have been capable of giving the hare a fair run and perhaps even catching the occasional one.

Qualities Required:
Speed
Agility
Stamina

Fox
Vulpes Vulpes
Length – 60 to 90cm Tail – 30 to 50cm
Weight – 5 to 10kg

The lithe, sinewy fox is one of nature's great survivors and has probably been hunted by man since its first attack on domestic poultry or lambs. Although regarded more as a pest than a sporting animal in the past, it did rise in estimation to be hunted with a good deal of pomp and ceremony by the foxhound packs. But it has also always been a quarry for coursing hounds and small though it is, it has large, needle sharp teeth, which it can bury to the gums through the muzzle of an attacking dog. Lurcher owners will tell you that few dogs have the courage to course fox consistently season after season. The fox, although not overly fast, can turn practically 90 degrees, or stop dead in full flight, making the hound overshoot, he also has great stamina and of course over familiar ground knows every nook and cranny where he can simply disappear, leaving the dogs looking utterly bewildered. Again, the smaller Irish greyhounds would have been best suited to fox.

Qualities Required:
Speed
Agility
Stamina
Courage (to a certain extent)

Wildcat
Felix silvestris grampia

Length – 56 to 76cm Tail – 28 to 38cm

Weight – 3.5 to 7kg

The wildcat is now confined to the remote areas of Scotland but, it is now thought, once also existed here in Ireland. The wildcat is certainly the most ferocious predator now existing in Britain and in the past terriers were sometimes used to bolt them, but if the cat could not or would not bolt that meant trouble for the terrier, lost eyes and ears bitten off or worse, was frequently the result. As a quarry for a coursing dog the wildcat with its limited turn of speed would scarcely be taxing, but when the dog did catch up, he would be confronted with a hissing, spitting, bundle of hair, teeth and claws. Only a dog with courage enough to go straight in and give a lethal bite could avoid punishment, the fencer would find itself being slowly cut up.

Any size of Irish greyhound would have been fit to catch a wildcat and would have had the guts and power to end things quickly.

Qualities Required:

Courage (to a certain extent)

Badger

Meles Meles

Length – 75 to 93cm

Height – 30cm

Weight – 10 to 18kg

The badger or 'grey' as he is often referred to in old documents was often classified along with the fox as vermin to be controlled; why this was so I do not readily understand as the badger is an inoffensive fellow. He will certainly eat poultry, but any that could be caught by a badger must have come to the end of the road anyway, the carcase has some uses, the skin when cured is extremely tough and durable and the fat was used in certain folk remedies, but the meat is apparently inedible. That he was hunted underground by terriers, is well recorded, but he was also pursued above ground by various breeds including coursing dogs, as can be seen from the following quote about an Earl of Eglinton in Scotland:

> '…and used moderate exercises, both coursing badgers, and hares with greyhounds on foot (before he was nobilitated), and afterwards frequently with hounds, hunting (on horses), the deer, and the fox in his woodlands yearly, at fittest seasons; and wolves when occasion offered.'

Of course a badger above ground would be ridiculously easy prey for a running dog and the tactic, once the catch was made, would be to pin the badger to the ground to prevent it turning and biting; the badger has a powerful bite as well as being extremely tough. This would have been an easy task for a dog of the size and power of the Irish greyhound.

Qualities Required:
Courage (to a certain extent)
Strength

Fallow Deer
Dama Dama
Length – 130 to 180m
Height – 50 to 120cm
Weight – 40 to 100kg
Fallow are not native to Ireland but were introduced by the Anglo-Normans as a favourite beast of the chase, which were more easily kept in parks than the native red deer. The earliest evidence for the arrival of fallow deer is in 1244, when 60 does and 20 bucks from Chester were stocked at Glencree, Co. Wicklow. Fallow, for

the most part would have been confined to the Anglo-Norman demesnes, except for escapees or gifts to the native Irish lords. The methods used to hunt them would have been similar to those used for red deer, it being the practice to use scent hounds to find the deer and then slipping the coursing hounds once within striking distance. Fallow are fast and strong, with a fair degree of stamina, but are nowhere near as formidable as the red deer.

The Irish greyhound would have had the speed, stamina and more than enough power to course fallow effectively.

Qualities required:
Speed
Stamina
Strength
Courage (to a certain degree)
Toughness

Red Deer
Cervus Elaphus
Length – 170 to 250cm
Height – 100 to 140cm
Weight – 70 to 200kg

The red deer was one of the principal animals of the chase here in Ireland, the legends tell us frequently of deer hunts, especially those concerning Finn MacCumhaill and his famous hounds Bran and Sceolaing.

That they were a formidable quarry is attested to in an eyewitness account of a hunt which took place in Scotland in the not too distant past, and was recorded by John Sobieski and Charles Edward Stuart in their book, *Lays of the Deerforest*.

'Two fine young dogs belonging to the late Glengarry were killed in their first run by a gallant stag which they were driving down the dry channel of a mountain stream and as they sprang at his throat from either side, with a rapid flourish of his head he struck them left and right and laid them dead amongst the stones.'

The dogs in question were Scottish deerhounds proving just how dangerous a stag could be, and again this was a highland stag, on average just over half the weight of the more powerful lowland animals, which would have represented the bulk of the Irish deer population.

The following is a graphic, eyewitness account of a stag course contained in Edward Jesse's, *Anecdotes of Dogs*. It took place on the Scottish island of Jura in August, 1835.

'The purest specimens of the deerhound now to be met with are supposed to be those belonging to Captain McNeill of Colonsay, two of them being called Buskar and Bran. And here let me give an extract from an interesting and graphic account, published by Mr. Scrope, of the performance of these dogs in the chase of a stag. Let us fancy a party assembled over-night in a Highland glen, consisting of sportsmen, deerstalkers, a piper and two deerhounds, cooking their supper, and concluding it with the never-failing accompaniment of whisky-toddy. Let us fancy them reposing on a couch of dried fern and heather, and being awoke in the morning with the lively air of 'Hey, Johnny Cope'. While their breakfast is preparing, they wash and refresh themselves at a pure mountain stream, and are soon ready to issue forth with Buskar and Bran. The party proceeds up a rocky glen, where the stalker sees a stag about a mile off. He immediately prostrates himself on the ground, and in a second the rest follow his example. We will not follow all the different manoeuvres of the deerstalker and his followers, but bring them at once near the unconscious stag. After performing a very considerable circuit, moving sometimes forwards and sometimes backwards, the party at length arrive at the back of a hillock, on the opposite side of which the stalker said, in a whisper, the deer was lying, and that he was not distant a hundred yards. The whole party immediately moved forward in silent and breathless expectation, with the dogs in front straining in the slips. On reaching the top of the hillock, a full view of the noble stag presented itself, who, having heard the footsteps, had sprung on his legs, and was staring at his enemies, at the distance of about sixty yards. The dogs were slipped; a general halloo burst from us all, and the stag, wheeling round, set off at full speed, with Buskar and Bran straining after him. The brown figure of the deer, with his noble antlers laid back, contrasted with the light colour of the dogs stretching along the dark heath, presented one of the most exciting scenes it is possible to imagine. The deer's first attempt was to gain some rising ground to the left of the spot where we stood, and rather behind us, but, being closely pursued by the dogs, he soon found that his only safety was in speed; and (as a deer does not run well up-hill, nor like a roe, straight down hill), on the dogs approaching him, he turned, and almost retraced his footsteps, taking, however, a steeper line of descent than the one by which he ascended. Here the chase became most interesting – the dogs pressed him hard, and the deer getting confused, found himself suddenly on the brink of a small precipice of about fourteen feet in height, from the bottom of which there sloped a rugged mass of stones. He paused for a moment, as if afraid to take the leap, but the dogs were so close that he had no alternative. At this time the party were not above one hundred and fifty yards distant, and most anxiously waited the result, fearing, from the ruggedness of the ground below, that the deer would not survive the leap. They were, however, soon relieved from their anxiety, for though he took the leap, he did so more cunningly than gallantly, dropping himself in the most singular manner, so that his hind legs first reached the broken rocks below; nor were the dogs long in following him. Buskar sprang first, and, extraordinary to relate, did not lose his legs. Bran followed, and, on reaching the ground, performed a complete somersault. He soon, however, recovered his legs, and the chase was continued in an oblique direction down the side of a most rugged and rocky brae, the deer, apparently more fresh and nimble than ever, jumping through the rocks like a goat, and the dogs well up, though occasionally receiving the most fearful falls. From the high position in which we were placed, the chase was visible for nearly half a mile. When some rising ground intercepted our view, we made with all speed for a higher point, and, on reaching it, we could perceive that the dogs, having got upon smooth ground, had gained on the deer, who was still going at speed, and were close up to him. Bran was then leading, and in a few seconds was at his heels, and immediately seized his hock with such violence of grasp, as seemed in a great measure to paralyse the limb, for the deer's speed was immediately checked. Buskar was not far behind, for soon afterwards passing Bran, he seized the deer by the neck. Notwithstanding the weight of the two dogs which were hanging to him, he continued dragging them along at a most extraordinary rate (in defiance of their utmost exertions to detain him), and succeeded more than once in kicking Bran off. But he became at length exhausted – the dogs succeeded in pulling him down; and though he made several attempts to rise, he never completely regained his legs. On coming up, we found him perfectly dead, with the joints of both his forelegs dislocated at the knee, his throat perforated, and his chest and flanks much lacerated. As the ground was perfectly smooth for a considerable distance round the place where he fell, and not in any degree swampy, it is difficult to account for the dislocation to his knees, unless it happened during his struggles to rise. Buskar was perfectly exhausted, and had lain down, shaking from head to foot much like a broken-down horse; but on our approaching the deer he rose, walked round him with a determined growl, and would scarcely permit us to get near him. He had not, however, received any cut or injury, while Bran showed several bruises, nearly a square inch having been taken off the front of his fore-leg, so that the bone was visible, and a piece of burnt heather had passed quite through his foot. Nothing could exceed the determined courage displayed by both dogs, particularly by Buskar, throughout the chase, and especially in preserving his hold, though dragged by the deer in a most violent manner.'

That the Irish greyhound was used to hunt stags is beyond question, in fact, red deer were probably their primary quarry, the qualities of deer ensured an exciting chase; they were fast, powerful, had a fair amount of stamina, and when turned at bay, a stag could be, as we have seen, a mighty foe. Deer, generally speaking would have had around 100 yards of law on the hounds, once the gap was closed the dogs would have tried to bring the deer down by seizing it by the leg to break its stride and bring it tumbling down, then it was a case of darting into the throat for the finishing hold. Large size is no real handicap in such a pursuit unless the size becomes so great that the dog loses its speed and stamina.

Qualities Required:
Speed
Stamina
Strength
Courage
Toughness

Wild Boar
Sus scrofa
Became extinct in Ireland in the early17th century.
Length – 90 to 180cm
Height – 65 to 100cm
Weight – 60 to 200kg

The wild boar, the most highly revered of Celtic animals, was famed for its strength and courage. The champion's portion at Celtic feasts, reserved for the greatest warrior, was the hind leg of a boar or pig. This wonderful animal, (I have to admit I am a fan), was the ultimate beast of the chase, it appears many times in Irish legend, always depicted as an animal of supernatural strength and ferocity, and the dogs to hunt them also had to be powerful and courageous. In old engravings and paintings of boar hunts, dead and dying dogs frequently appear because, as the artist Ridinger stated:

> 'This is the most comical but also the most dangerous of hunts, because a wild pig is such a dangerous animal that it spares neither man, horse, nor dog.'

Another old saying from the past was that, 'if you want boars heads you must use dogs heads,' referring to the high mortality in a boarhound pack.

Randle Cotgrave of French-English dictionary fame, (1611), gives this explanation of the word, 'jaque.'

'A Jacke, or coat of maile; and thence, a Jacke for the body of
an Irish greyhound, &c.; made commonly of a wild Boares
tanned skinne, and put on him when hee is to coape with that
violent beast.'

Many men have been killed hunting boar through the ages as a
result of being caught in a charge, dying as a result of the femoral
artery being severed, or worse still, disembowelled. That horses
can be severely wounded by boar is evident in a story my father
told me. He relates that as a boy he knew a farmer who had a
large 'Landrace' boar, which had not had its tusks removed and
one day it struck a horse, which was sharing the same paddock.
The horse's hind leg had been sliced open so badly it had to be
put down. I myself have seen footage of a wild pig hunt in the
southern states of America, here the hunters use trail hounds to
bring the pig to bay and then medium sized American bulldogs
or pit bull terriers to go in and seize. In one segment of the
footage a boar had been brought to bay in a shallow creek with the
hounds noisily baying all around and darting in now and again
at the boar's rear to keep it busy. The boar meanwhile chomped
its jaws in anger and spun round, turning this way and that, to
protect itself, in the midst of doing this one hound got itself out
of position and the boar 'hooked' it. The dog was thrown into
the air and performed a complete somersault before landing in
the water, a short time later the hound could be seen floating off
down river. Truly the boar deserves its mighty reputation. The
wild boar was fast, immensely powerful and ferocious, a real test
for the Irish greyhound.

Qualities Required:
Speed
Stamina
Strength

Courage

Toughness

Wolf

Canis Lupus

Became extinct in Ireland at the beginning of the 18th century.

Length – 100 to 150cm Tail – 50cm

Height – 60 to 90cm

Weight – 30 to 70kg

It is hard to imagine that this amazing animal once roamed throughout Ireland, indeed so plentiful were they at one time that another name for Ireland was 'Wolf Land'. But, once England gained control an active programme of extermination began, which was achieved in two ways, firstly, by habitat destruction, by clear-felling the great forests of Ireland and then by paying large bounties for every wolf killed. The wolf was portrayed as a disciple of the devil and a monster to be destroyed, but he fell victim to the biggest monster of all, 'Man'. Indeed, it pains me to think of those last few wolves, starving, in a devastated landscape, with every man's hand turned against them.

The wolf, it would seem, was never really a popular beast of the chase, there is no mention in Irish legend of epic wolf hunts, unlike the deer and the boar and it was certainly not favoured in medieval Europe either. In many cases the wolf was only hunted when absolutely necessary, Anglo-Saxon kings actually sentenced criminals to hunt wolves as a punishment and King Edgar, (r. 959-975), commuted the tax of gold and silver imposed upon the Welsh for an annual tribute of 300 wolf heads.

Russia appears to be the only country where wolf hunting was carried on with any degree of enthusiasm and it was as a form of pageantry by the aristocracy, involving maybe 100 or more of their wolfhounds, the Borzoi, with dozens of hunt attendants and still more scent hounds. One method involved using the scent hounds to track the wolf and then slipping the Borzoi once in range. When the wolf had been brought to bay, the hunters would come up and either shoot the wolf or net it alive, in order that it could be released again to provide sport another day.

A brief description of a Russian wolf hunt is given in an article dated Feb. 9th, 1907 from, *The Rider and Driver – An Illustrated Weekly of Outdoor Sport*, written by Joseph B. Thomas, Jr., an American, who was in Russia to buy a brace of Borzoi.

'The most common method of hunting is in connection with a guanchi (foxhound) pack.

As a rule, 20 Borzoi, i.e., 10 leashes, make a hunt. The leashes being held by the hunters, mounted on Khirgez ponies at allotted stations silently awaiting the game, which is driven from the woods by the foxhounds. At sight, the leashes are slipped and a wild race for life and death takes place. In the case of wolves being caught and held by the dogs, the hunter throws himself from his mount and with a clever thrust from his long Caucasian dagger puts and end to further resistance.

The finest dogs from a show standpoint are not spared from this work, and in every instance I found these working dogs perfectly kind even with strangers, in spite of all foolishness and gibberish that has been written to the contrary.

Trusting that what I have been enabled to ascertain may throw light on many a mooted question, and may be the means of advancing the breed in England and America, and inviting anyone who may desire further information to do me the honor of looking over my collection of photos, I remain,

Very truly yours,

Joseph B Thomas, Jr.,

Valley Farms Kennel, Simsbury, Conn.'

The wolf's unpopularity as a sporting animal stems from several factors; firstly, the wolf is not a dangerous animal to hunt, (not for the humans involved anyway), a wolf will never attack a man unless it has been cornered and has no other option, the same cannot be said of the boar and stag, an enraged boar will attack anything which presents itself as a target, stags can be extremely dangerous too, just a few years ago a farmed stag here in Ulster killed its keeper. Danger and excitement were important parts of the hunt, exciting stories of near misses could be told and retold round the fires and in the halls of our ancestors. The danger involved has made the wild boar a popular quarry since time immemorial to the present day.

Secondly, a wolf hunt seldom had a quick resolution, the wolf has extraordinary stamina and can lope along at a good speed for miles on end, therefore the necessity of getting as close as possible before slipping the coursing hounds; the Irish greyhound would have been much faster than the wolf with its initial speed but if it failed to catch within the first few hundred yards, the wolf would more than likely have got away. And of course there is the problem of getting within a couple of hundred yards of the wolf, wolves have excellent hearing, vision and sense of smell, not an easy animal to approach unnoticed.

Nicholas Cox in his, *Gentleman's Recreation*, of 1674 gives a detailed description of how wolves were hunted in Europe in his day and it is likely the method used in Ireland would have been very similar.

'There is no Beast which runneth faster than the Wolf, and holdeth wonderfully also. When he is hunted with Hounds he flieth not far before them; and unless he be coursed with Grey-hounds or Mastiffs, he keepeth the Covert like the Bear or Boar, and especially the beaten Ways therein. Night is the usual Time of his preying, though Hunger will force him to prey by Day. They are more subtle are crafty (if more can be) than the Fox or any other Beast: When they are hunted, they will take all their advantages, at other Times they will never run over-hastily, but keep themselves in Breath and Force always.

A Wolf will stand up a whole Day before a good Kennel of Hounds, unless that Grey-hounds or Wolf-dogs course him. If he stand at bay, have a care of being bitten by him; for being then mad, the Wound is desperate, and hard to be cured.

When a Wolf falls into a Flock of Sheep, with his good will he would kill them all before he feed upon any of them, and therefore all means should be used to destroy them, as by hunting at Force, or with Grey-hounds or Mastiffs, or caught in Gins and Snares, but they had need be strong. For Encouragement to the meaner Sort in Ireland, whosoever took a sucking Whelp, or preying Cub, a Dog or a Bitch-Wolf, and brought the heads of either to the next Justice of Peace, for Reward for the first, he received twenty Shillings; for the second, Forty; for the third five Pound; and for the last, six Pounds: Which late Encouragement hath in a manner cleared that Kingdom of them.

They bark and howl like unto Dogs; and if there be but two of them together, they make such a terrible hideous Noise, that you would think there can be no less than twenty of them in a Body.

When any one would Hunt the Wolf, he must Train him by these means: First let him look out some fair Place, a mile or more from the great Woods, where there is some close standing, to place a Brace of good Grey-hounds in, if need be, the which should be closely environed, and some Pond of Water by it: There he must kill a Horse that is worth little, and take the four Legs thereof, and carry them into the Woods and Forrests adjoining; then let four men take every Man a Leg of the Beast, and draw it at his Horse-tail all along the Paths and Ways in the Woods, until they come back again to the place where the Carcase of the said Beast lieth; there let them lay down their Trains. Now when the Wolves go out in the night to prey, they will follow the cent of the Train till them come to the carcase where it lieth. Then let those who love the Sport, with their Huntsmen come early and privately near the Place; and if they are discernible as they are feeding, in the first place let them consider which Way will be the fairest Course for the Grey-hounds, and place them accordingly, and as near as they can let them forestall with their Grey-hounds the same way that the Wolves did or are flying either then or the Night before; but if the Wolves be in the Coverts near the Carrion that was laid for them to feed upon, then let there be Hewers set round the Coverts to make a Noise on every side but only that where the grey-hounds do stand; and let them stand thick together, making what noise they can to force them to the Grey-hounds: Then let the Huntsman go with his Leam-hound, and draw from the Carrion to the Thickets Sides, where the Wolves have gone in, and there the Huntsmen shall cast off the third part of their best hounds; for the Wolf will sometimes hold a Covert a long Time before he will come out.

The Huntsmen must hold near into the Hounds blowing hard, and encouraging them with their Voice: For many Hounds will strain Courtesie at this Chase, although they are strong and fit for all other Chases.

When the Wolf cometh to the Grey-hounds, they who hold them will do well to suffer the Wolf to pass by the first Rank until he come further, and let the last Rank let slip their Grey-hounds full in the face of the Wolf, and at the same Instant let all the other Ranks let slip also: So that the first Rank staying him but ever so little, he may be assaulted on all Sides at once, and by that means they shall the more easily take him.'

Cox makes the following mention about Irish greyhounds.

'...commonly called Wolf-Dogs...they are in great Estimation, and much sought after in Foreign Parts, so that the King of Poland, (John III), makes use of them in his hunting of great Beasts by Force.'

Hunting 'by force', means an active pursuit of game, whether to run it down with scent hounds, coursing hounds or both.

He also details a different method of hunting, one which would seem to me to have chiefly been employed to fill the larder rather than pursue a specific prey.

'In Poland, when the King hunts, his Servants are wont to surround a Wood, though a Mile in Compass, with Toyls which are pitched on firm Stakes. This being done, the whole Town, all Sexes and Ages, promiscuously rush into the Inclosure, and with their loud shouts rear all the Beasts within that Wood; which making forth, are intercepted in the Nets. There small and great Beasts are intangled together, after the same manner, as when amongst us we draw a Net over a Pond, and after beating it all over with Poles, we bring out not only Pike and Carp, but lesser Fry; so they inclose at once Deer, Boar, Roe-buck, and Hare: For so they order their Nets, that the space of those Meshes which are twisted with greater Cords, for the entangling of greater Beasts; that Space, I say, is made up with smaller Whip-cord, for the catching smaller Prey.

He hath a great Race of English Mastiffs, which in that Country retain their Generosity, and are brought up to play upon greater Beasts. It is not counted amongst them disagreeable to the Laws of the Chase, to use Guns.'

Speed was not required in this form of hunting so we see the use of mastiffs as seizing dogs to pin big game such as boar and deer for the hunter to despatch.

There is an interesting article in *The Field*, 7th February, 1891 telling us more of the wolf hunt in Russia.

'The wolfdog in the south of Russia, near Jassy, is much larger than the Borzoi. A perfect wolfdog must run up to a wolf, collar him by the neck just under the ear, and with the two animals rolling over, must never lose his hold, or the wolf would snap him through the leg. Three such dogs hold the wolf powerless so that he can be muzzled and taken alive. The biggest Scotch deerhounds have been tried and found wanting, as they will not hold long enough. The Russian dogs stand thirty-two inches at the shoulder, are enormously deep through the girth, have a roach back, very long and muscular quarters, capital legs and feet, great length and power of jaw, a very profuse coat of soft, silky texture, but somewhat open. In my presence a noted dog was set to show how one could perform single-handed. The wolf got a start of two hundred yards, the dog after six hundred yards had him by the neck, and both seemed to turn head over heels in a mass. Next two dogs were slipped at a wolf, caught him one on each side by the neck, and held him till he was muzzled.'

There is yet another reference to how the wolf was hunted in an

WHAT WERE THEY USED FOR?

article by A. Croxton Smith which appeared in *Country Life*, 27th December, 1924.

'Hunting the wolf in the sixteenth century was carried out much in the same manner as it was in Russia when the nobles had their packs of borzois, and could organise the sport on a grand scale: that was by beating the coverts and driving the quarry towards the hounds stationed on the outskirts in the open country. Great pains had to be taken, however, in the old days to ensure that the wolves should lie up where they were wanted, a bullock being killed as a bait and the four legs dragged for some distance through the wood towards the carcass, so that as the animals went out to feed at night they would strike the trail and follow it to the dead body. Many precautions were observed in order to lull the suspicions of the wolves. Unnecessary trouble was caused because the lords and nobles who followed the sport were not accustomed to rise as early as was desirable. One may read all about it in Turberville's translation of, *'The Noble Art of Venerie or Hunting'*, commonly known as, *'The Book of Hunting'*, (1575). The translator, explaining why the chapter was included in an English work, remarks:

'The wolf is a beast sufficiently known in France and other countries where he is bred; but here in England they be not to be found in any place. In Ireland, (as I have heard), there are great store of them; and because many noble men and gentlemen have a desire to bring that country to be inhabited and civilly governed, (and would God there were more of the same mind), therefore I have thought good to set down the nature and manner of hunting at the wolf according to mine author.'

But, let us say that the Irish greyhound closed with the wolf, what

209

was he up against? Well, the wolf, although slight in build, is a very powerful animal and is equipped with large teeth and an extremely powerful bite; to illustrate this point I shall quote Dutch Salmon.

'What would it take to kill a wolf? I don't know. But I've seen a 90 pound female, caught in a leghold trap and frothing mad, take down a stand of one inch thick alder brush clip, clip, clip, with her teeth, till the area for six feet around was mowed clear. No dog I'd ever own would ever be allowed near such an animal, unless I wanted rid of the dog.'

A formidable opponent without doubt! Although the Irish greyhound was a very formidable canine and the vast majority would have outweighed the wolf, I think it is safe to say that they would generally have been run in pairs at a wolf, a one on one contest would have resulted in quite a bit of damage to the dog, even during the few minutes it would have taken for the hunters to catch up.

Qualities Required:
Speed
Stamina
Strength
Courage
Toughness

Hunter or Status Symbol?

The title of this piece represents a query which kept running through my head as I read the physical descriptions of Irish greyhounds by eyewitnesses. Most talked of dogs of gigantic size, though there were exceptions and then we have the detailed measurements of one of the Marquis of Sligo's dogs. What became clear to me was that the Irish greyhound must have come in a wide variety of sizes over the years. It's my belief that in the great hound's heyday it would have varied between 28 and 34 inches at the withers, with the occasional larger specimen. One has to remember that all things have an optimum size and to go beyond this spells trouble; the optimum size for a working Borzoi was given as 30 inches, a Scottish deerhound 28 to 30 inches and the German boarhound, 28 inches. Now remember, these were performance-bred dogs, not the size someone thought they should be. Salmon stated that the maximum size for a coursing hound should be 32 inches and 120lbs and he certainly knew what he was talking about. Beyond this size, speed, stamina and agility all drop off sharply; remember, coursing hounds are the formula one cars of the dog world, it is their job to catch fast and elusive prey.

So where did all the huge four feet high, (at the top of the head), Irish hounds come from? Well, it is my belief that there were probably two sizes of Irish greyhound, one being the hunting dog par excellence which had existed for centuries and the other an even larger version which was bred more for appearance and as a household guard. We can see a precedence for this in ancient Assyria where bas-reliefs show mastiffs used in the hunt, powerful but athletic animals and other images showing much larger and heavier mastiffs which would have been of little use on the hunting field but would have made imposing and formidable guards.

The Irish greyhound was exclusively in the hands of the ruling class and became as much a sign of their status as a good horse, fine clothes or a luxurious dwelling. We see from the twelfth century on, their increased export to generate revenue and their use as gifts with which to curry favour among the nobles of Europe. In latter days they almost became too valuable to risk in the hunting field and the one thing, which would make them even more impressive was an increase in size. I remember some twenty or more years ago seeing a large Great Dane bitch up close and being wowed by its enormity. The Irish nobles went for the same effect both by breeding off the largest individuals and feeding up with nourishing food. Goldsmith was of the same opinion when he wrote of a four-foot specimen:

'His eye was mild, his colour white, and his nature seemed heavy and phlegmatic. This I ascribe to his having been bred up to a size beyond his nature; for we see in man, and all other animals, that such as are overgrown are neither so vigorous nor alert as those of more moderate stature. The greatest pains have been taken with these to enlarge the breed, both by food and matching.'

The Irish wolfhound and Great Dane of today are, I believe, as large as dogs have ever been and we have looked at the effectiveness of the wolfhound on the coursing field in chapter one. Dogs of such size are just too big and awkward to course well. I do believe however, that a 36 inch, Irish greyhound would have performed much better than a wolfhound of the same size because it would be bred from pure performance stock and was more greyhound-like in build and indeed would have been much gamer, (more willing).

To sum up then, the traditional quarry of the Irish greyhound was big game, the red deer, wild boar, wolf and in later days, fallow deer. All required a dog with speed, stamina, strength, courage and toughness; that the dogs possessed these attributes is confirmed by their fame throughout Europe and further afield. In reality, the Irish greyhound was more commonly used as a deerhound than a wolfhound.

The later dogs of the 17th and 18th centuries I feel, began to suffer through a diminishing genepool, (their rarity is frequently reported at this time), disuse, and by being selectively bred for large size rather than performance, becoming more of a status symbol than a hunting dog.

CHAPTER SIX

WHY AND HOW WAS THE IRISH GREYHOUND CREATED?

The Irish greyhound, basically a larger, much more powerful, and much more ferocious form of the common greyhound. Why was there a need for such an animal and when was it created? The origins of the great hound are lost in antiquity, the first written mention we have of them is in the letter of Symmachus in 391, indicating that they were already an established Irish breed. So how did they come to be in Ireland? Were they developed here from existing breeds, or were they brought in by traders or settlers from elsewhere in Europe?

One could theorise that the Celts brought these dogs to Ireland during their invasion, where, in later times they became known as an Irish breed. However, there is no real proof of any such invasion taking place, the term, 'Celt' itself, is a very general term, which was used to describe people from modern day Turkey, across Europe to Spain, in much the same way as, 'barbarian' and 'Scythian' were also used by Greeks and Romans to describe anyone outside their own world. I have no doubt though that the ancient Irish and Britons traded on a regular basis with their European cousins, and that these large coursing hounds could have found their way here on trade ships. There is one thing wrong with this theory though, in that, if the breed, which became the Irish greyhound was simply a European breed, bred in Ireland, then why did they become so highly sought after and indeed why did they cease to exist in Europe? We know from eminent European naturalists writing in the 17th century that the Irish greyhound was distinct from any other breed of dog in Europe and highly-valued. What I do believe is that the coursing dogs of the so-called Celts did play a role in the development of the great Irish hound. The Roman name for the fastest Celtic hunting dog was the 'Vertragus', which sounds very much like our modern greyhound; to quote Arrian:

'There is nothing more beautiful to see, whether their eyes, or their whole body, or their coat and colour…The neck should be long, round and flexible. Wide chests are better than narrow ones. The legs should be long, straight, and well-knit, the ribs strong, the back wide and firm without being fat, the belly well drawn up, the thighs hollow, the tail narrow, hairy, long and flexible with thicker hairs adorning the tip. The feet should be round and firm. These hounds may be of any colour.'

And again.

'In appearance they are splendid animals, the best bred of them, with fine eyes, fine bodies all over, fine coats and fine appearance. They should be long from head to tail, and the eye prominent, large and bright that should astonish the man who sees them.…The colour makes no difference, whatever it may be, not even if the hounds are black or tan or white all over.'

This breed was used for hare coursing, a sport Arrian was deeply enamoured of.

'For one does not take hounds out in order to catch the beast, but for a race and competition, at least if one is a true sportsman.'

There are powerful greyhound-like dogs hunting wild boar, depicted on frescoes in the Mycenaean palace of Tiryns in Greece, dating from 1400 to 1125 BC. So, there appear to have been two types of greyhound in ancient times, the swifter more delicately made dog used to course the hare, ancestor of the modern greyhound, and a larger, more powerful dog used to hunt large game such as deer and boar.

Were these greyhound types kept pure once in Ireland and simply bred larger and more powerful to develop the Irish greyhound or was other blood added, and if so, what could this outside blood have been, say prior to 300 AD?

The Contemporary Breeds

There are a few modern day British dogs, which are thought to have existed prior to or since Roman times.

The Greyhound
The most famous Celtic breed, known to the Romans as the 'vertragus.'

The Scottish Deerhound
Caius, in his work of 1577, described greyhounds as coming both smooth and 'shake-haired,' so evidently the two breeds were closely allied and separated mainly by coat type.

The Whippet

The remains of small greyhounds, (whippets), have been found among the artefacts of Corbridge, Roman Station on Hadrian's Wall.

The Mastiff

It is said to have been found in Britain by the Romans, though there are some doubts about this now, but whatever the truth, it is believed they were resident during the Roman occupation of Britain.

The Cairn Terrier

Generally thought to be the oldest terrier breed, how old is not certain, but it does bear a striking resemblance to the 'Coventina terrier', a Romano-British artefact dating back to the third century.

The Kerry Beagle

This is one of Ireland's oldest breeds and her only scent hound. How old is uncertain, but beagles are mentioned in the Irish legends which go back to and pre-date the Roman occupation of Britain.

As I see it there are three possibilities as to the origins of the Irish greyhound:

Firstly, they were the pure descendants of the larger coursing hounds bred by the Celtic peoples, imported to Ireland and preserved here, while they dwindled and were crossed with, and amalgamated by other breeds in the rest of Britain and Europe.

Secondly, they were the large Celtic coursing hounds crossed with another breed or breeds to increase their strength.

Thirdly, they were a breed which originated in Ireland by crossing locally sourced varieties together.

Without proper scientific testing it is of course impossible to say which, if any of these theories is correct, but they would seem the most likely alternatives.

Personally speaking, I think the third option is the most plausible for the following reasons:

Firstly, the breed was described as an Irish one as early as the fourth century and they appear in Irish mythology in events going back to the first century AD.

Secondly, from the Middle Ages onward, Irish greyhounds came to be much sought after in Britain and the rest of Europe, indicating that they were indeed indigenous to Ireland.

Lastly, towards the end of the eighteenth century when the breed was becoming extinct, no other country claimed to have pure Irish greyhounds and it was said that the breed could not be maintained at their best outside of Ireland.

So, if this is the case, why did the Irish create such a breed and how did they do it? We have already looked at the breeds which were probably extant in Britain at this time, these would also have most likely been in Ireland, or available to the Irish through trade. To get inside the mind of the ancient Irish you merely have to keep in mind the old saying, 'necessity is the mother of invention.' Basically you start with the problem and find a way of solving it. As regards coursing this is graphically illustrated by today's hunters, a modern courser selects his dog according to his quarry and even the type of country he is running the dog over. For organised hare-coursing events such as the 'Waterloo Cup', the dog of choice was the greyhound, these contests were and still are in Ireland ran over large, flat, open expanses of farmland and for this quarry, terrain and the rules involved, the greyhound reigned supreme.

But, for coursing typical countryside, practically no coursing man uses pure-bred greyhounds, instead they use greyhound-crosses known as, 'lurchers' or 'longdogs' and they themselves are known as 'lurchermen'. There are various reasons for this, one of the reasons, believe it or not is that they are too fast. The greyhound of today is faster than it has ever been, this can be demonstrated by comparing the times of the top modern track racers with those of the past. Such tremendous speed is of course essential to win the top events of the racetrack, but the terrain and obstacles of the countryside are very different footing. Damaged feet in the form of 'knocked-up' toes and torn pads would be all too common, broken bones and lacerations from collisions and high speed tumbles would also shorten the greyhound's working life. Another problem with the greyhound is again directly related to their speed, they tend to be short on stamina, because a greyhound works so hard, it rapidly builds up high levels of lactic acid in the muscles, so they are perhaps only capable of half the runs in a day or night's coursing that a lurcher could manage. One last thing I shall mention, which is also probably the most important reason that the greyhound is not used by luchermen, and to be fair it seems universal with the sighthound breeds, is a lack of intelligence or trainability if you will. A greyhound if it misses its initial target has the tendency to look around for another and if that means disappearing over the hill or into the next field then that is what it will do, regardless of how loudly you shout or whistle to bring it back. This to a lurcherman is the ultimate sin, it will completely ruin a day's coursing or a night's lamping, scaring all the game off the land as well as elevating his blood pressure to dangerous levels!

But, having said all that, the greyhound is the rock upon which all lurchers are built, it is after all the fastest breed of dog on earth and speed is the number one requisite in catching fast and elusive game. The majority of lurchers, are usually three-quarter greyhound and one-quarter something else, though sometimes the first crosses work well enough. What the other blood is depends entirely on the quarry. Over time the working Border collie cross has undoubtedly been the favourite, contributing intelligence, hardiness and stamina to the blend, all desirable attributes for a pot filler, which historically is what a lurcher was. However, when we examine the crosses which have been bred for specific quarry, other breeds appear in the mix. In the fens and flat, open country areas of England, the hare is the favoured quarry and here the greyhound is often merged with another sighthound, the Saluki, (it is these sighthound to sighthound crosses which are known as longdogs), Salukis are renowned for their stamina, (for a sighthound breed), and the resulting dog has a speed/stamina blend which makes it the ideal hare courser in open country. Intelligence doesn't seem to be one of the criteria here.

The fox is another quarry which tests the lurcher in a different way, here courage becomes much more important in the equation. Blends of all kinds have been used as fox dogs but today by far the most popular is the bull terrier cross. The bull terrier used is the Staffordshire bull terrier or nowadays much more commonly the American pit bull terrier. This blend gives courage, stamina and strength, although the bull usually has to be diluted to one quarter for best results.

So, to return to the Irish greyhound, a breed created to hunt red deer, wild boar and, when necessary, wolf, let us remind ourselves of the qualities required:

Speed
Red deer and wolf can run very fast, wild boar can also be very fast especially over short distances, so speed is an essential quality.

Stamina
Both boar and especially deer hunts would require dogs with excellent stamina and the wolf's stamina is legendary. Running over rough terrain, through dense cover, falling, being thrown, regaining their feet, taking hold and finally bringing the quarry down or to a halt, straining every muscle and sinew, would severely tax a dog's stamina.

Strength

Red deer and boar are big, powerful animals which are hard to stop, so any dog used to hunt them needs to have great strength.

Courage

Dogs used to hunt red deer and boar are tackling much larger animals than themselves, this takes courage, but when you combine this with the degree of punishment they can receive, then you need very courageous animals indeed. Dogs which will stay in the fight even when badly injured.

Toughness

Red deer, especially stags can severely punish attackers, dogs have been killed by a single blow from a stag's antlers and wild boar are legendarily formidable, again capable of killing a dog with a single blow of their tusks. Wolves too, have a very powerful bite which can do serious damage. Dogs used to hunt these animals have to be extremely tough and capable of withstanding severe punishment.

The greyhound was too delicate to hunt the stag, boar or wolf on their own and the mastiff was too slow to catch consistently. The Irish wanted a dog which could meet all these criteria and so they sought to create one. Let us remind ourselves of the breeds of dog available to them according to archaeological finds and written accounts:

The vertragus or greyhound
The rough-haired greyhound/Scottish deerhound
The whippet
The mastiff
A rough-haired terrier type dog, not unlike a Cairn terrier
A scent hound, possibly like the Kerry beagle

Due to their small size, the whippet and the terrier can be ruled out straightaway, the scent hound too can be ruled out as the Irish greyhound was to be a running dog to catch game, not sniff them out. That leaves the rough and the smooth greyhound and the mastiff. Let us look at the qualities provided by each:

Greyhound: Speed
Mastiff: Strength, Courage, Toughness

And the blend of the two would have more stamina than either pure breed.

When we hear the term mastiff today, we think of the huge, heavy, lethargic, panting animals exhibited at Crufts etc. The original mastiff, the one which existed up into the 18th century was a very different kettle of fish. It was smaller, much lighter in build, with a smaller head, tighter skin and altogether was a much healthier and much more athletic animal. It was closely allied to the bulldog, indeed the two were considered the same breed separated mainly in point of size. The term 'bulldog' itself was first mentioned in 1632, prior to this both large and small dogs were simply referred to as mastiffs.

This, original mastiff was the fighting dog 'par excellence' of its day, it was used for all manner of baiting sports, dog-fighting, hunting dangerous game and as a guard or war-dog. It was strong, tough and the most courageous breed of dog known. In short, the ideal breed to blend with the greyhound.

In, *The Chase* by Gaston de Foix, 1387, and later translated by Edward Duke of York, there is an interesting description of three varieties of 'alaunt', which was basically another name for the mastiff.

'And the good Alaunts are those which men call 'Alaunts gentle' (that is, well-bred Alaunts)... Gentle Alaunts should be made and shaped as a greyhound, in all things except for the head, which should be great and short. And although there are Alaunts of all colours, the true colour of a good Alaunt, and that which is most common, is white with black spots about the ears, small eyes, and white ears standing up with sharp points.

The other kind of Alaunt is called 'veuterere'. They are shaped almost like a greyhound, they have a great head, great lips and great ears, and with such dogs, men aid themselves in baiting the bull, and at hunting the wild boar… And when they can overtake a beast they bite it and hold it fast, but by themselves they could never take a beast unless greyhounds were with them to make the beast slow down.

The other kind of Alaunt is the Alaunt of the butchery, such that you may see in large towns. They are called great butchers' hounds, and the butchers keep them to help them bring in their beasts that they buy in the country, for if an ox escape from the butchers that lead him, his hounds would go and take and hold until his master had come, and should help him to bring it to the town again… They are good for bull-baiting and for hunting wild boar.'

From this information it would seem that the alaunt 'veuterere' was the standard mastiff and that the alaunt of the butchery was the dog which would become known as the bulldog. The alaunt gentle however, was much more greyhound-like, except in head and indeed sounds not unlike the Irish greyhound. It is possible that this variety of alaunt contained the blood of the Irish hound, the best alaunts were said to come from Spain, and Ireland carried on regular trade with Spain from before this time. It is of course also possible that some of this alaunt gentle blood was taken back to Ireland and there infused into the Irish greyhound.

Regarding size I shall quote from Goldsmith's *Animated Nature* of 1770.

'The wolf from the tip of the nose to the insertion of the tail is about three feet seven inches long, and about two feet five inches high; which shows him to be larger than our great breed of mastiffs, which are seldom found to be above three feet by two.'

So, the mastiff was typically twenty-four inches at the shoulder, perhaps occasionally reaching twenty-six inches, this is the dog I believe was used to cross with the greyhound to produce the Irish greyhound. Edward Jesse, in his *Anecdotes of Dogs* (1846), was of the same opinion.

Irish Greyhound. 1820. Said to be from, The Natural History of Beasts, Birds and Fishes.

'In the pictures of Rubens, Snyders, and other old masters, some of the powerful dogs there represented would appear to be a breed between the greyhound and mastiff. Nothing can exceed the majestic and commanding appearance of these dogs, and such a breed would be most likely to produce the sort of animal most capable of contending with the wolf.'

To help with size our forefathers would have crossed greyhounds, probably both rough and smooth, with the larger mastiffs and then to achieve a faster animal, bred back into the greyhound side again. Once this was done it was merely a matter of breeding from the best performers. Over time a new breed would evolve that was not quite as fast as the pure greyhound but which was bigger, much more powerful, tougher, more intelligent, much more courageous and a good deal more ferocious.

This blend produced a dog which effectively combined the best qualities of the greyhound and mastiff. A dog, ideal for hunting stag or boar, the primary Irish beasts of the chase, but which could be pressed into service against the wolf if necessary, and one which made a formidable guard or war-dog as well.

CHAPTER SEVEN

RECREATING THE IRISH GREYHOUND

We now know without a doubt that the Irish greyhound became extinct early in the nineteenth century. The wild boar had disappeared in the seventeenth century, the wolf had become extinct in the eighteenth century, and red deer were teetering on the verge. The landed gentry to whom he had almost exclusively belonged seemed to have lost interest in the breed and as such the great hound of Ireland slipped quietly into the realm of legend.

For me this seems like a terrible loss, to lose one of the most famous breeds of dog ever to have existed, and it started me thinking, what if we could bring them back? Skulls have been recovered from ancient sites here in Ireland so maybe with the miracles of modern science it would be possible to retrieve DNA and discover the genetic code of the Irish greyhound. I know that there is ongoing research in Europe where they are attempting to bring the aurochs back from extinction, an endeavour I wish them every success with. I believe that where the extinction of a species has been caused by man then it is right to bring it back if we can, but where an animal has become extinct naturally, such as the woolly mammoth, then there is no just reason to bring them back, let the dead remain with the dead.

The drawback of DNA research and trying to bring an animal back in this way is that it is extremely difficult to do and is extremely expensive. To refer again to the aurochs, scientists have fully sequenced the genome of a 6,700 year old specimen which they then compared with existing breeds of domestic cattle. They compiled a list of thirty-four primitive cattle breeds based on their closeness to the aurochs. From these, six cattle breeds were selected to be used in a 'back-breeding' programme to recreate the aurochs, though they did leave out the fighting bull of Spain, a close ancestor, due to concerns about aggression, a mistake in my opinion. Their efforts, seen in what are called, 'Tauros' cattle are impressive. They look quite aurochs like, are healthy, hardy and independent, just a bit lacking in size, but it is still quite early days.

Why couldn't the same thing be done for the Irish greyhound? I believe it could, now admittedly we don't have any Irish greyhound genome to use as a base, but I really don't think we need it anyway. From the research I carried out into how the Irish greyhound was created it seemed most likely that only two breeds of dog were required, the common greyhound and the mastiff. The greyhound is still very much with us and there is a plentiful supply of performance bred animals, either for the track or coursing. We also have the English mastiff, but today's breed has been bred for showing for many years and has, as every dog breed bred for show purposes, had certain traits exaggerated. Heads have been made larger, bone size increased, massive bodies encouraged, loose skin increased and I have never seen one that wasn't obese. The result is a dog devoid of athleticism that suffers from a wide variety of health problems. As I have said before, the mastiff of today is a very different animal from the original mastiff of antiquity. Plus the modern mastiff has had other breeds added to it over the last two hundred years or more, such as the bloodhound, the Tibetan mastiff, and the Saint Bernard. Indeed back in the day almost any large dog was used to bolster the diminishing gene pool. And of course there are no performance bred English mastiffs today.

So the mastiff of old is gone, what do we do now? Well, actually the original mastiff bloodline is still with us. As a result of research I have carried out over many years on the mastiff bloodlines in general, I have discovered the purest mastiff bloodline of all, and it is the breed known today as the game-bred American pit bull terrier. The blood actually exists in another two breeds, the Staffordshire bull terrier and the American Staffordshire terrier as all three breeds originate from the same stock, but only the game-bred pit bull is performance bred. But how can a terrier be a mastiff? Well, that's a story for another time, or maybe another book, for now, you'll just have to trust me on this. Okay, but what is a game-bred American pit bull terrier? Today in America and other countries around the world, pit bulls have become fashionable so much so, that any dog resembling a pit bull these days is given the name, (just take a look at, 'YouTube' and you'll see what I mean). As a result there are many dogs called pit bulls which maybe don't contain any pit bull blood at all. A 'game-bred' pit bull, is essentially one with a pedigree that comes from a long line of performance bred stock. Historically this meant dogfighting, but today also applies to lines used to hunt wild pig and these dogs are one hundred percent, performance bred, canine athletes with all the qualities of the mastiff of antiquity.

So, the performance bred greyhound is our foundation, it is the fastest of all dogs, supremely healthy and genetically is probably the most perfect dog breed in the world. Now I know greyhounds have a fair bit of courage, but the courage we need here is an extreme kind that will cause a dog to tackle larger, stronger opponents and continue the struggle even if badly wounded.

Speed has been taken care of, that leaves stamina, strength, courage and toughness, and the performance bred American pit bull terrier can provide all four attributes to a superlative degree. They have great stamina, are pound for pound the strongest of all dogs, in weight-pull events worldwide the breed consistently beats sled dogs. They are the most courageous breed of dog in the world. Throughout its history it has been used not just for dogfighting, but for bull and bear baiting, the hunting of dangerous game and as catch dogs for unruly boars and bulls. Pursuits which require them to attack animals many times their own size and to withstand terrific punishment without giving up the fight. Incidentally, the exact same pursuits the mastiff of old was used for, and needless to say, they are incredibly tough. Courage will also make a dog run harder for longer, that is why Lord Orford bred fighting bulldogs into his greyhounds in the eighteenth century.

No other breeds would be necessary in my opinion. The pit bull is of course known everywhere thanks mainly to sensationalist and usually wildly inaccurate media coverage, which depicts them as something of a blend between the cartoon 'Tasmanian devil' and the Tyrannosaurus Rex! I think the name itself contributes to the problem, 'pit bull' sounds ferocious and lends itself well to horror stories, I doubt if the breed would grab the same attention if it was known as the 'Yankee Terrier', a name put forward in the days when breeders first sought registration with one of the Kennel Clubs in America. The truth is the pit bull terrier is generally speaking, a very docile, easy-going animal with people, and can be the same with other animals. If broken to them by a responsible owner, they are no more a liability than any other powerful dog. The problem, as always, lies with the owner, the unfortunate thing is that the garbage peddled by the media only encourages the delinquent brigade, (people who shouldn't be allowed to own a goldfish never mind a dog), to get the breed and then they encourage the dog to attack everything in sight. The pit bull, although illegal in the

United Kingdom is legal in the Irish Republic where, incidentally, attacks on people are practically unheard of. Having come into personal contact with several different individuals of the breed I have always found them to be very docile and indeed affectionate animals, only too willing to be petted or have an ear scratched.

They are indeed a remarkable animal and are almost on a par with the greyhound as being the most genetically perfect of dogs. An added benefit of just using two breeds to recreate the Irish greyhound is that we will be able to have them coming uniform in qualities and appearance all the sooner, as there will be less variation in the gene pool.

Our recreated Irish greyhound then will be a mix of the performance bred greyhound and performance bred pit bull. It is usual in a mating of this kind to put the pit bull dog over the greyhound bitch. The size of the offspring depends a lot on the size of the individuals bred from, but typically they would be around the twenty-five inch mark at the shoulder. If greater speed were required it would simply be a matter of breeding into the greyhound once more, the bull blood is typically reduced to one quarter. This also intends to increase the height up to twenty-six to twenty-eight inches. But, they'd be too small I hear you say. Not at all, I believe dogs of this breeding and stature run in pairs would be capable of taking wolf. Notice I said 'pairs' and 'taking wolf'. I do not believe it would have been the norm in the past to run single dogs at a wolf, nor do I believe the dogs were expected to kill the wolf unassisted. Certain exceptional dogs may have been capable of killing a wolf one on one, but it is a safe bet that they would take a fair bit of damage in doing so. I think the accounts given of Russian wolf hunts give a pretty accurate idea of how wolf hunts would have been carried out in Ireland.

If larger dogs were required over time then it would simply be a matter of breeding from the larger individuals as long as they were proven performers and sound. Though I do not believe there would be any real need to breed dogs much more than thirty inches at the shoulders.

To quote Salmon on the subject:

'Sized right, say 31 inches at the withers and 110 lbs, such a hound would be a swift, bone-crushing beast of a hunter.... 32 inches and 120 lbs should be the outer limit for acceptable size!'

The Irish greyhound recreated in this way would be every bit as formidable a canine as the original breed and could be used, (if they were around and it was legal), to hunt red deer, wild boar and wolf.

The method detailed above, I believe, is very close to how the Irish greyhound was created. The originators of course had far fewer breeds of dog to utilise than are available today, but in the breeds they did have, they had all the components necessary to create the ultimate coursing hound for big game.

But what if we didn't limit ourselves to performance breeds? I was asked by an historian some years ago when discussing the Irish greyhound as to how I would go about creating a modern facsimile so to speak. A dog which would look like the original but not be expected to be as gifted a hunter as the original. As I see it there are two options:

Using my own beliefs on the subject, we could mate a performance bred greyhound dog to an English mastiff bitch, (or similar). The first generation would likely come too heavy and so one of the bitches would need to be bred back to the greyhound side once again to reduce the mastiff blood to one quarter. At this point I believe the offspring would be starting to look very similar to the original Irish greyhound and of course would be very large, impressive dogs. The greyhound blood would make them much healthier, more athletic animals and increase their prey drive, but needless to say they would not be on a par with the original Irish greyhound in the hunting field, though they may make formidable guard dogs.

A second option would be to take a big, sound Great Dane bitch and mate her to a performance greyhound dog. My reasons for choosing the Great Dane are that it is not a million miles away from the Irish greyhound to begin with. It appears to be a blend of mastiff and coursing hound already. Like the mastiff it is large and smooth-coated but it is a much more athletic breed, though it does have its health issues too. I also have a sneaking suspicion that the Great Dane probably contains a little Irish greyhound way back in its pedigree. Unlike the mastiff cross, I believe the offspring from this mating would straightaway be very close in appearance to the Irish greyhound. Again, they would not be on a par with the original breed as hunters but would certainly be imposing canines and possibly effective bodyguards as well.

Of course using either of these options it would be necessary to select the healthiest, most athletic mastiff or Great Dane bitch you could find.

What I am going to do now is something, which I am fairly certain has never been done before and that is to draw up a breed standard for the Irish greyhound. Why draw up a standard for a dog which no longer exists? Well, I feel an exercise like this gets me closer to my subject and can often prove enlightening.

IRISH GREYHOUND/WOLFDOG STANDARD

General Appearance

The Irish greyhound is a larger, more powerful version of the common greyhound, it combines great power, speed and athleticism.

Characteristics
Of great power, activity, speed and courage.

Temperament
Gentle and kind to family and friends, reserved with strangers.

Head and Skull
The frontal bones of the forehead slightly raised, the skull broader and deeper than any other coursing hound. Muzzle long, moderately pointed, but deeper and more punishing than any other coursing hound.

Eyes
Any colour and alert.

Ears
Not of great importance but preferably rose type, like a common greyhound.

Bite
Scissor bite.

Neck
Long, very strong and muscular.

Forequarters
Sloping shoulders, very powerful and muscular. Elbows turned neither inwards nor outwards. Legs, straight with good bone, strong.

Body
Chest, fairly broad and deep. Back, strong and of good length. Loins arched slightly with belly well drawn up.

Hindquarters

Very muscular thighs, extremely powerful, strongly boned and turning neither outwards nor inwards.

Feet

Strongly made with good bone, toes well arched and closed, nails strong and curved and turning neither inwards nor outwards.

Movement

Fluid and surprisingly light for the size of the dog.

Tail

Long, slightly curved, of moderate thickness and well covered with hair.

Coat

Short, smooth and glossy.

Colour

Black, brindle, red, fawn or any of these colours mixed with white or pure white. Nose black.

Weight and Size

The minimum height and weight of dogs should be 30 inches and 100 lbs, of bitches 28 inches and 85 lbs. There is no maximum upper size limit so long as the dog is both active and sound, however, the Irish wolfdog is an athlete and a coursing dog first and foremost, therefore, I would recommend that dogs should not exceed 36 inches at the shoulders.

CONCLUSION

In Search of the Irish Wolfhound has been a personal project of mine which has taken the best part of twenty years to complete. I worked on it when I had the time and more importantly, the inclination, and there were long gaps when I didn't put pen to paper, or rather fingers to keyboard. For the last few years it has been 'almost finished', this is a very dangerous mindset for any writer and tends to encourage an overconfident lethargy, for me anyway. I assumed I could polish it off in two or three weeks if I really hunkered down, (I can be dangerously optimistic!), and so things dragged on and I got preoccupied with another project until August of 2022 when I found renewed vigour to finally finish this book and remove the psychological anchor which I feel I have been carrying way too long. Today, I finally feel that I can leave down the load, the book is written!

So, why did I write this book? Well, I have always been fond of dogs and keenly interested in all breeds, but like most people I have a shortlist of breeds I am especially interested in, and one of these is the Irish wolfhound. I read about how they were used to hunt wolf, deer and the giant Irish elk, though this last prey would have been a bit tricky as they were extinct several thousand years before there was such a thing as an Irish wolfhound. But then I became aware of a controversy where some people claimed that George Graham didn't save the Irish wolfhound from extinction but merely created a new breed and called it the Irish wolfhound. This piqued my interest, though it was quite a while before I really started looking into it, but when I did I was hooked, if I had realised how much time and effort I was going to lavish on the project I would have stopped immediately, but ignorance is bliss, so I kept going and all these years later here I am.

What did I discover? Well, the truth, which to me is an important virtue, even if it can be painful, as my parents used to say to me on occasion, 'tell the truth and shame the devil'!

And the truth is as we have seen, that the Irish wolfhound we know and admire today is largely the creation of one man, George Augustus Graham, and is basically a blend of Great Dane and Scottish deerhound. Why did Graham give his new breed the name of Irish wolfhound? I myself think there are two possibilities, firstly, that Graham believed the Irish wolfdog was simply a bigger, more powerful version of the Scottish deerhound and set out to recreate such a dog, and secondly, that Graham knew he was creating a new breed but sought to take the name and history of the old breed for his own creation. I am inclined to favour the first option. As we have seen, in every contemporary description and artwork I found, the Irish greyhound or wolfdog was smooth-coated, without exception. How Richardson and Graham missed this in their research, if they did any, I do not know. Though maybe it was a case of the old saying, 'There are none so blind as those that will not see'.

When the 'resuscitated' wolfhound was revealed to the public, his contemporaries poured scorn on him letting him know the original was smooth-coated and challenging him to reveal where he sourced his stock. But, as time went by memories faded and more people were drawn to the imposing new breed and as another saying goes, 'when enough people believe a lie, it becomes a fact'. As the twentieth century progressed, all knowledge of the old breed disappeared and the new breed became the dog of Irish legend.

Now I fully realise that a lot of Irish wolfhound breeders and owners will probably not be too happy with my findings. But, does it really matter if the Irish wolfhound of today is not the original breed? That fact doesn't change the dog of today one iota. It is still the same huge, shaggy, impressive dog. It still has the same wonderful temperament and gentle disposition. The dog I have owned for the last nine years is a mix of four different breeds, essentially a mongrel, but she is loyal, obedient, a good watchdog, loves children and has helped me through very difficult times. Would an ancient pedigree make me think more highly of her, not really, it is the dog I own I care about, not some distant ancestor.

I shall finish with a personal appeal to Irish wolfhound breeders. Breed only from the healthiest, soundest stock and spay anything that falls short so that they can't influence the gene pool. Don't get carried away with size for the sake of size, health is number one. A great way of exercising your dogs and testing for soundness is to course artificial lures set up in a field, the dogs love it and it is great fun and a good way for owners to meet up. By breeding from only the finest individuals, the Irish wolfhound will be spared the fate of so many pedigree dogs that have been turned into physical wrecks, for the sake of grossly exaggerated breed points, with no thought seemingly given to the dog's happiness and welfare.

In closing, I wish nothing but success to the Irish wolfhound, long may it prosper.

CHRONOLOGY

50   The sons of Uisnech flee from Ulster to Scotland taking one hundred and fifty hounds with them.

391   The Roman Consul, Quintus Aurelius Symmachus sent a letter to his brother Flavinius, thanking him for the gift of seven Irish dogs.

420   Saint Patrick and Irish hounds aboard ship.

780   An alternative date for the *Dog of Montargis* story, during the reign of Charlemagne.

995?   King of Norway acquires an Irish hound which he names Vige.

1000   Icelandic, *Saga of Burnt Njal.*

1014   Soldiers fighting for Brian Boru at Clontarf compared to wolfdogs.

1201   King John, order at Portsmouth to Henry Fitzwarin to find accommodation for his Irish hounds.

1210   King John gives his son-in-law, Prince Llewellyn of Wales an Irish greyhound, which he names Gelert.

1224   King of Connaught, Hugh O'Connor and Mac Branan, Steward of Hounds.

1280   Edward I orders hounds from Ireland.

1335   Edward III sends huntsman, Reginald to retrieve nineteen hounds from Irish Lords.

1371   Traditional date of combat between Aubrie de Montdidier's greyhound and its master's murderer, Macaire.

1409   *The Annals of Ulster*, record that Richard Burke died after having his leg broken by an Irish greyhound.

1533   King Charles V of Spain is painted with what appears to be an Irish greyhound by Titian.

1535   Philip Roche of Kinsale sends brace of Irish greyhounds to Thomas Cromwell.

1539   Irish greyhound taken to America by Hernando de Soto.

1545   Request to Henry VIII by a Spanish nobleman for four Irish greyhounds yearly.

1562   Two Irish greyhounds presented to Elizabeth I by Shane O'Neill, through the Earl of Leicester.

1571   Edmund Campion writes of Irish greyhounds in his, *A History of Ireland*.

1585   Deputy of Ireland, Sir John Perrott, sent a brace of Irish greyhounds to Sir Francis Walsingham.

1586   William Camden describes the Irish wolfhound in his, *Britannia*.

1587   Emmery de Lew requests an Irish greyhound from Lord Willoughby.

1591   Sir Brian O'Rourke arrived in Glasgow with four Irish greyhounds for James VI, later James I of England.

1593   Four Irish greyhounds accompanied Grace O'Malley when she went to see Elizabeth I.

1595   Letter to the Earl of Essex from, Henry the Great, of France requesting a pair of Irish greyhounds.

1596   Spanish poet, Lope de Vega, wrote sonnet about the Irish greyhound.

1605   Sir Arthur Chichester letter to Lord Cranbourne about getting him Irish greyhounds and breeding some.

1606   Chichester sent more Irish greyhounds to Cranbourne.

1608   Irish greyhounds sent to Gilbert Talbot by Captain Esmond.

1612   Story of Lady Marian and the Massarene Wolfhound.

1615   Presentation of Irish greyhounds to the Great Mogul, Jahangir, by Sir Thomas Roe.

1620   Alathea Howard, daughter of Gilbert Talbot, painted with an Irish greyhound by Rubens.

1623   Duke of Buckingham's request to Lord Falkland for white Irish greyhounds.
        Six Irish greyhounds sent as a gift to the French King, Louis XIII.

1633   First portrait of Thomas Wentworth with an Irish greyhound by Van Dyck.

1639   Second portrait of Thomas Wentworth with an Irish greyhound by Van Dyck.

1641   Cardinal Richelieu presented with Irish greyhounds.

1646   Papal Nuncio, Rinuccini, writes of Irish greyhound given to him.

1652   Decree issued banning the exportation of Irish greyhounds from Ireland by Oliver Cromwell.

1653   Dorothy Osbourne writes to Sir William Temple and Henry Cromwell, she received a pair of young Irish greyhounds from Cromwell.

1654   Sir James Ware writes of wolfdogs in his, *Antiquities of Ireland*.
        Christopher Wase writes about Irish greyhounds in his translation of the *Cynegeticon* by Grattius.

1657   Viscount Conway involved in the trade of Irish greyhounds.

1660   Mrs Catherine Philips wrote a poem about an Irish wolfdog.

1662   Earl of Winchelsea gifted two Irish greyhounds to Sultan Mehmed IV at Constantinople.

1667   Dogfight between an Irish greyhound and a mastiff in front of Charles II.

1669   John Evelyn; dogfight between an Irish greyhound and a mastiff in the Bear Garden.

1675   *The Gentleman's Recreation,* by Nicholas Cox, mentions the Irish wolfdog.

1678   The Earl of Ossory intends to present a trio of Irish greyhounds to the King of Spain and another trio to the King of Sweden.

1680   Sir Neil O'Neill painted with an Irish greyhound by John Michael Wright.

1685   3rd Earl of Inchiquin painted with an Irish greyhound by Sir Godfrey Kneller.

1689   Rev. T. Ovington writes of wolfdogs presented to the Persian Emperor.

1691   *The Dog of Aughrim.*

1697   Ray describes the Irish greyhound as the 'greatest dog.'

1698   John Dunton writes of Irish greyhounds in his, *Teague Land: A Merry Ramble to the Wild Irish.*
An alderman of Cork talks of a lack of wolves.

1710   Last Irish wolf killed at Annascaul in County Cork.

1735   Linnaeus refers to the Irish greyhound as 'Canis Hibernicus'.

1738   German naturalist, Ridinger, makes an engraving of an Irish greyhound.

1748   Harris speaks of wolfdog scarcity and compares to the mastiff.

1750   The Lord Lieutenant of Ireland, Lord Chesterfield, writes a letter detailing his efforts to procure Irish greyhounds but, that they had become extremely rare and difficult to obtain.
2nd Earl of Altamont painted with an Irish greyhound by Thomas Gibson.

1774   *Animated Nature*, by Oliver Goldsmith in which he gives a detailed description of the Irish greyhound.

1775   *A Tour in Ireland,* by Richard Twiss describes Irish greyhounds.
Buffon describes Irish greyhounds in his, *Natural History.*

1779   Gabriel Beranger, an artist, describes the Irish greyhounds of Lord Altamont.

1785   Painting of Irish greyhound by Schreber.

1789   Gough, in his edition of Camden's *Britannia*, says maybe not ten wolfdogs left in Ireland.

1790   One of eight remaining Irish greyhounds is measured by A.B. Lambert.
Woodcut by Thomas Bewick of an Irish greyhound in his, *General History of Quadrupeds*.

1803   Irish greyhound mentioned in the, *Sportsman's Cabinet*, by William Taplin.

1818   Curwen in his, *Observations on the State of Ireland*, stated the Altamont wolfdogs were gone and that the breed was extinct.

BIBLIOGRAPHY

Aelian, *De Natura Animalium* (circa 200)

Arrian, *The Cynegeticus* (London, J. Bohn, 1831)

Ash, Edward C., *American Kennel Gazette* (October 1938)

Ash, Edward C., *The Book of the Greyhound* (London, Hutchinson & Co., 1933)

Bally Shannon, *Country Life (November* 1918)

Barnard, Toby, *Making the Grand Figure* (Yale University Press, 2004)

Barros, Joao de, *Decades of Asia* (1552-1563)

Barton, Frank Townend, *The Kennel Encyclopaedia* (London, Virtue & Co. Ltd., 1903)

Barton, Richard, *A Dialogue Concerning Some Things of Importance to Ireland* (Dublin, S. Powell & Oli Nelson, 1751)

Bell, Thomas, *A History of British Quadrupeds* (London, John Van Voorst, 1837)

Bentley, Richard, *Bentley's Miscellany Vol. 16* (London, R. Bentley, 1844)

Berwick, Edward, *The Rawdon Papers* (London, John Nichols and Son, 1819)

Bewick, Thomas, *A General History of Quadrupeds* (Newcastle upon Tyne, 1790)

Bingley, Rev. William, *Memoirs of British Quadrupeds* (London, Darton and Harvey et al, 1809)

Bingley, Rev. William, *Nature, Vol. III, Fifth Edition* (London, Baldwin & Cradock, 1831)

Bowers, Fredson T., *American Kennel Gazette* (May 1st 1939)

Bowles, William, *An Introduction to the Natural History of Spain* (Madrid, 1775)

Brookes, Richard, *A New and Accurate System of Natural History* (London, T. Carnan & F. Newbery, 1772)

Brown, Thomas, Capt., *Anecdotes of Dogs* (Edinburgh, Oliver & Boyd, 1829)

Bruce, John, *Calendar of State Papers, Charles I, 1634-35* (London, Longman, Green, Longman, Roberts and Green, 1864)

Buffon, Comte de, *Natural History* (London, J.S. Barr, 1792)

Camden, William, *Britannia* (1586)

Campion, Edmund, *A History of Ireland* (1571)

Carson, Ciaran, *The Tain* (London, Penguin, 2007)

Clayton, Knight & Moore, *The Expedition of Hernando de Soto to North America in 1539-1543 Volumes 1 & 2* (University of Alabama Press, 1995)

Compton, Herbert, *The Twentieth Century Dog* (London, Grant Richards, 1904)

Cotgrave, Randle, *A Dictionarie of the French and English Tongues* (1611)

Cox, Nicholas, *The Gentleman's Recreation* (London, J. Wilcox 1721)

Curwen, J.C., *Observations on the State of Ireland* (London, Baldwin, Cradock and Joy, 1818)

Dalziel, Hugh, *British Dogs* (London, The Bazaar, 1879)

DaSent, Sir George Webb, *The Story of Burnt Njal* (London, Longman, Green, Longman & Roberts, 1861)

Dawson, Major A.J., *Everybody's Dog Book* (London, Collins, 1922)

Donovan, Edward, *Natural History of British Quadrupeds, Vol. I* (London, R. Gilbert, 1820)

Drummond, W.H. Rev., *Biography of Archibald Hamilton Rowan* (Dublin, Thomas Tegg & Co., 1840)

Dublin University Magazine Vol. LVI (Dublin, William Robertson, 1860)

Dublin University Magazine Vol. XVI (Dublin, William Curry, Jun. and Company 1840)

Duke of York, Edward, *The Master of Game* (1406-1413)

Dunton, John, *Teague Land: A Merry Ramble to the Wild Irish* (1698)

Dyer, Walter A., *Country Life in America* (January 1916)

Dyer, Walter A., *The Great Hound of Ireland* (Country Life, February, 1920)

Evelyn, John, *Diary and Correspondance* (London, Henry Colburn 1850)

Fairley, J.S., *An Irish Beast Book* (Belfast, Blackstaff Press, 1975)

Foix, Gaston De, *Livre de Chasse* (1387)

Gibson, C.B., *The Last Earl of Desmond* (Dublin, Hodges and Smith, 1854)

Glenmasson Manuscript, Táin Bó Flidhais (15th century)

Goldsmith, Oliver, *A History of the Earth and Animated Nature* (London, J. Nourse, 1774)

Goodrich, S.G., *A Pictorial History of France* (Philadelphia, E.H. Butler & Co., 1861).

Gough, Richard, *Camden's Britannia* (London, T. Payne & Son, 1789)

Gregory, Lady, *Gods and Fighting men* (London, J. Murray, 1904)

Grubb, Jonathan, *The Zoologist Vol. 20* (London, John Van Voorst, 1862)

Guthrie, William, *Geograhical Grammar* (London, 1770)

Harting, J.E., *The Irish Wolfhound, Baily's Magazine of Sports & Pastimes Vol. XXXIV* (1879)

Hayes, Edward, *The Ballads of Ireland, Vol. II* (London, Edinburgh and Dublin, A. Fullerton & Co., 1857)

Hickman, G.W., *The Irish Wolfhound* (The Livestock Journal, March 1881)

Hogan, Rev. Edmund, *The History of the Irish Wolfdog* (Dublin, Sealy, Bryers & Walker, 1897)

Holinshed, Raphael, *The Chronicles of England, Scotland and Ireland* (London, John Harrison, 1577)

Jardine, Sir William, Bart., *Natural History of Dogs* (London, Henry G. Bohn, 1865)

Jesse, Edward, *Anecdotes of Dogs* (London, Henry G. Bohn, 1858)

Jesse, George R., *Researches into the History of the British Dog* (London, Robert Hardwicke, 1866)

Johnson, T.B., *The Sportsman's Cabinet, Vol. I* (London, Sherwood, Gilbert & Piper, 1833)

Jones, Arthur Frederick, *American Kennel Gazette* (February 1928)

Jones, Arthur Frederick, *American Kennel Gazette* (January 1929)

Karunanithy, David, *Dogs of War* (London, Yarak Publishing, 2008)

Kinsella, Thomas, *The Táin* (Oxford University Press, 1970)

Knolles, Richard, *Turkish History* (London, Jonathan Robinson, 1687)

Lawless, Valentine, 2nd Baron Cloncurry, *Personal Recollections of the Life and Times* (Dublin, James McGlashan, 1849)

Le Miroir (June 7th 1917)

Lee, Rawdon Briggs, *Modern Dogs* (London, Horace Cox, 1893)

Leighton, Robert, *Dogs and All About Them* (London, Cassell and Company Ltd., 1910)

Leighton, Robert, *The Complete Book of the Dog* (Cassell and Company Ltd., 1922)

Leighton, Robert, *The New Book of the Dog* (London, Cassell and Company Ltd., 1907)

Linnaeus, Carl, *Systema Naturae* (Holland, Johan Willem Groot, 1735)

Lloyd, Freeman, *Dog Breeds of the World, American Kennel Gazette* (1931)

Macpherson, James, *The Works of Ossian* (Paris, Valade & Barrois, 1783)

Mansson, Olaf, *A History of the Northern Peoples* (Rome, 1555)

Marples, Theo, *Show Dogs-Their Points and Characteristics* (Manchester, Our Dogs, 1908)

Maxwell, W.H., *The Field Book* (London, Effingham Wilson, 1833)

McComb, William, *Guide to Belfast etc* (Belfast, William McComb 1861)

Morgan, Lady Sydney, *O'Donnel* (London, Henry Colburn, 1814)

Murphy, E. & McCormick, F. *The Faunal Remains from the Inner Ditch of Haughey's Fort, Third Report* (Belfast, Queen's University, 1991)

Murphy, Eileen, *Medieval and Post-Medieval Butchered Dogs from Carrickfergus, Co. Antrim, Northern Ireland* (Belfast, Queen's University, 2000)

Newman, Edward, *The Zoologist, Vol. XX* (London, John Van Voorst, 1862)

O' Flaherty, Roderic, *A Chorographical Description of West or H-Iar Connaught* (1684)

Oddy, Boycott H., *Country Life* (May 15th 1909)

Our Friend The Dog, *The Mentor Vol. 6 No.16* (October 1st 1918)

Ovington, Rev. John, *A Voyage to Surat in the Year 1689* (London, Jacob Tonson, 1696)

Parliamentary Gazetteer of Ireland (Dublin, A. Fullerton & Co., 1846)

Parr, Richard, *Life of Ussher* (London, Nathanael Ranew, 1686)

Parry, Edward Abbott, *Letters from Dorothy Osborne to Sir William Temple 1652-1654*, (London, J.M. Dent & Sons Ltd., 1888)

Pegge, Rev. Samuel, *Archaeologia, Vol. 10*, (1792)

Pennant, Thomas, *British Zoology* (London, Benjamin White, 1777)

Percy, Sholto and Reuben, *The Percy Anecdotes, Vol. IX* (London, J. Cumberland, 1826)

Pliny the Elder, *Naturalis Historia* (77)

Plutarch, *De Sollertia Animalium (Moralia)* (975-985 BC)

Polyaenus, *Strategems* (163)

Public Record Office, *Calendar of State Papers, Domestic Series, Charles I 1634 – 1635 Vol. VII* (London, Longman, Green, Longman, Roberts and Green)

Purchase, F.H., *Some Early Illustration of the Old Irish Wolf-Dog, 1738-1839* (The Kennel, 1911-1912)

Raikes, Charles, *The Englishman in India* (London, Longmans, Green and Co., 1867)

Richardson, H.D., *Dogs; Their Origin and Varieties* (Dublin, James McGlashan, 1847)

Richardson, H.D., *The Irish Penny Journal Vol. 1, No. 45* (May, 1841)

Ridinger, Johann Elias, *Enturfweiniger Thiere Volume 1* (Augsburg, 1738)

Scharff, R.F., *The Irish Naturalist* (August & September, 1924)

Schreber, Johann Christian Daniel, Die Säugthiere in Abbildungen nach der Natur, (Erlangen, 1774)

Scott, Ralph Montague, *The History, Character and Description of the Irish Wolfhound* (Irish Wolfhound Association, 1925)

Shaw, Vero, *The Illustrated Book of the Dog* (London, Cassell, 1881)

Smith, A. Croxton, *Country Life* (May 1932)

Smith, A. Croxton, *Country Life* (September 20th 1919)

Smith, A. Croxton, *Sporting Irish Wolfhounds* (Country Life, December 1924)

Smith, A. Croxton, *The Dogs that Fingal Bred* (Country Life, October 1914)

Smith, A.Croxton, *Kennel Notes* (1912)

Smith, Charles, *The Ancient and Present State of the County and City of Waterford* (Dublin, A. Reilly, 1746)

Smith & Meyrick, *The Costume of the Original Inhabitants of the British Islands* (London, R. Havell, 1815)

Sobieski & Stuart, *Lays of the Deer Forest* (W. Blackwood & Sons 1848)

Stanihurst, Richard, *Description of Ireland* (1586)

Starbuck, L.O., *Ireland's Great Hound* (Country Life, February, 1929)

Stewart, Jacqueline Archer, *American Kennel Gazette* (June 30th 1925)

Stonehenge, *The Dog in Health and Disease* (London, Longman, Green, Longman and Roberts, 1859)

Stuart, James, *Historical Memoirs of the City of Armagh* (Newry, Alexander Wilkinson, 1819)

Taplin, William, *The Sportsman's Cabinet* (London, J. Cundee, 1803)

The Annals of the Four Masters (17th century)

The Annals of Ulster (15th century)

The Book of Leinster (12th century)

The Book of Lismore (15th century)

Sturluson, Snorri, *The Heimskringla* (1225)

The Natural History of Quadrupeds and Cetaceous Animals (Bungay, Brightly & Co., 1811)

The Penny Magazine (November 1840)

The Speckled Book (15th century)

The Sporting Magazine, Vol. 26 (London, J. Wheble, 1805)

The Ulster Journal of Archaeology, Vol. 7 (Belfast, Archer & Sons, 1859)

Thomas, Joseph B., *The Rider and Driver-an Illustrated Weekly of Outdoor Sport* (Feb 9th 1907)

Thompson, William, *The Natural History of Ireland, Vol. IV* (London, Henry G. Bohn, 1856)

Topsell, Edward, *History of Four-Footed Beasts* (London, William Laggard, 1607)

Traille, Jean de la, *Discours Notable Des Duels* (Paris, Claude Rigaud, 1607)

Transactions of the Linnean Society, Vol. III (London, J. Davis, 1797)

Trapman, A.H., Captain, *The Dog, Man's Best Friend* (London, Hutchinson & Co., 1929)

Turberville, George, *The Noble Art of Venerie or Hunting* (London, C. Barker, 1575)

Turner, Alfred, *Irish Wolfhounds in Tierra del Fuego* (The Kennel Gazette, March 1916)

Twiss, Richard, *A Tour in Ireland 1775* (London, J. Robson &c, 1776)

Urban, Sylvanus, *The Gentleman's Magazine, Vol. II* (London, William Pickering; John Bowyer Nichols and Son, 1834)

Walker, Joseph Cooper, *Historical Memoirs of the Irish Bards, Volume II* (1818)

Ware, Sir James, *Antiquities of Ireland* (London, 1654)

Wase, Christopher, *Cynegeticon* (Charles Adams, London, 1654)

Watson, James, *The Dog Book* (New York, Doubleday Page & Co., 1905)

Williams, Rev. Charles, *Dogs and Their Ways* (Routledge, Warne & Routledge 1863)

Wood, Thomas, *An Inquiry Concerning the Primitive Inhabitants of Ireland* (London, G. & W.B. Whittaker, 1821)

Youatt, William, *The Dog* (New York, Leavitt and Allen, 1857)